DAVID WILLIAMSON'S
ARIA

CURRENCY PRESS
The performing arts publisher

ENS
THEATRE E
MB E
ML E

CURRENT THEATRE SERIES

First published in 2025
by Currency Press Pty Ltd,
Gadigal Land, Suite 310, 46–56 Kippax Street, Surry Hills, NSW 2010, Australia
enquiries@currency.com.au
www.currency.com.au

in association with Ensemble Theatre

Typeset by Brighton Gray for Currency Press.

Front cover shows Tracy Mann; cover photography by Brett Boardman.
Cover design by Alphabet Studio.

Currency Press acknowledges the Traditional Owners of the Country on which we
live and work. We pay our respects to all Aboriginal and Torres Strait Islander Elders,
past and present.

A catalogue record for this
book is available from the
NATIONAL LIBRARY OF AUSTRALIA
National Library of Australia

Contents

Aria was first produced by Ensemble Theatre, Cammeraigal Country, Kirribilli, on 24 January 2025, with the following cast:

CHARLIE	Rowan Davie
CHRISSY	Suzannah McDonald
DANIEL	Sam O'Sullivan
JUDY	Danielle King
LIAM	Jack Starkey-Gill
MIDGE	Tamara Lee Bailey
MONIQUE	Tracy Mann

Director, Janine Watson
Assistant Director, Anna Houston
Set and Costume Designer, Rose Montgomery
Lighting Designer, Matt Cox
Composer and Sound Designer, David Bergman
Operatic Voice Coach, Donna Balson
Stage Manager, Lauren Tulloh
Assistant Stage Manager, Bella Wellstead
Costume Supervisor, Renata Beslik

CHARACTERS

MONIQUE, *late 60s*
CHARLIE, *39*
MIDGE, *27*
LIAM, *42*
CHRISSY, *40*
DANIEL, *42*
JUDY, *41*

MONIQUE, *in her late sixties, looks around her elegant and spacious living room. On the table in a silverware ice bucket are bottles of French champagne waiting to be opened and plates of canapés waiting to be eaten. She checks that everything is in place and circles around the room looking at the huge framed photos of her three sons, Charlie, Liam and Daniel, all taken by a professional portrait photographer. Smaller photos are family shots of her sons with their wives, Charlie with his ex-wife Penny and their two children, and Liam with Chrissy and their four children, and Daniel with Judy and their one child.* MONIQUE *is still an elegant and arresting woman with a commanding almost imperial presence and is dressed in an expensive and tasteful outfit. This is obviously a big occasion for her. The doorbell rings and she darts expectantly just offstage to the front door of her apartment and lets in her youngest son,* CHARLIE. CHARLIE *is 39, tall, handsome and athletic. He's extroverted and easy-going and everyone likes him. He's certainly the apple of* MONIQUE*'s eye. She ushers him eagerly inside and hugs him.*

MONIQUE: Charlie, so wonderful to see you. Mothers don't have favourite sons of course, but if they did I'd have to admit you were mine.

> *She hugs and kisses him.*

Don't ever tell your brothers I said that.

CHARLIE: They knew. Liam spent most of his early years trying to murder me.

MONIQUE: I still have nightmares about the time he held your head underwater in the bath.

CHARLIE: I still have panic attacks when I snorkel.

MONIQUE: He was such an aggressive little brute from the get-go. If the milk wasn't flowing fast enough he'd punch me in the nose. And Daniel …

CHARLIE: Daniel's a good guy.

MONIQUE: Lovely boy …

> *She sighs.*

But spark, he lacked spark. You always had spark.

CHARLIE: Okay, Liam … I still have trouble with Liam, but Daniel—

MONIQUE: They're both fine now, it's just they weren't up to much when they were little. Where's Midge?

CHARLIE: Sulking in the car.

MONIQUE: What about this time?

CHARLIE: She asked me how she looked and I said 'great' and she yelled that I was lying and her dress was horrible and she started belting me with her handbag.

MONIQUE: I tried to warn you.

CHARLIE: I know she's high maintenance, but at her best—

MONIQUE *snorts dismissively.*

MONIQUE: She has a 'best'?

CHARLIE: She's great … fun.

MONIQUE *nods.*

MONIQUE: I see her having 'fun' on Facebook. Endless selfies of brain-dead, shrieking young tarts, drinking cocktails stuffed full of green foliage.

CHARLIE *nods.*

CHARLIE: Her friends are pretty shallow.

MONIQUE: If you want depth, don't marry a beautician.

CHARLIE: She's surprisingly smart.

MONIQUE: Charlie! If the purpose of life is to wade into the great ocean of human wisdom, Midge and her friends have barely got their toes wet.

CHARLIE: Mum, give her a chance.

MONIQUE: You've always been so streetwise? How could you decide to marry someone you'd barely met?

CHARLIE: The minute we laid eyes on each other there was electricity like you wouldn't believe.

MONIQUE: It might be 'Hallelujah Chorus' between the sheets but my God what a price you're going to pay.

CHARLIE: She's made me feel alive again.

MONIQUE: Darling, it's called lust. I've experienced it myself from time to time, and you act on it, fine, but the last thing you do is marry what causes it.

CHARLIE: Mum, give her a chance.

MONIQUE: Have you straightened it out with Penny about access to your girls?

CHARLIE: She's still playing hardball.

MONIQUE: The one time she let you have them, your lovely Midge sent them home with half-up, half-down e-girl bright-purple hairstyles.

CHARLIE: Which they loved.

MONIQUE: They're six and eight!

CHARLIE: Okay. I'm working on it.

MONIQUE: Please get it resolved. I want to see my grandchildren.

CHARLIE: It'll work out. She just needs more time.

> MIDGE, *27, sweeps in looking surly. She's very attractive and knows it and is dressed in a short skirt.* MONIQUE *puts on a forced smile.*

MONIQUE: Midge.

> *They air kiss awkwardly.*

That's a very … colourful dress.

MIDGE: It's totally mank!

MONIQUE: Mank?

MIDGE: Disgusting, vile.

MONIQUE: You chose it.

MIDGE: I asked Charlie to check it out and he lied.

CHARLIE: I didn't. I like it!

MIDGE: Then what bloody use are you!

> *She moves straight across to the champagne that's already open and helps herself defiantly to a full glass and chomps on a canapé and stares back balefully at the two of them.* MONIQUE *turns to* CHARLIE.

MONIQUE: Will you make sure the champagne keeps flowing, darling?

CHARLIE: It will. Excuse me for a moment.

> MONIQUE *moves across to* MIDGE *as* CHARLIE *absents himself in the direction of the bathroom.*

MONIQUE: Midge, I know that things didn't get off to a great start between us.

MIDGE: And that's my fault?

MONIQUE: It's nobody's fault.

MIDGE: Really? Your wedding speech? 'Midge has the kind of assets very few men can resist, and Charlie—

She imitates MONIQUE*'s sigh.*

—was no exception.'

MONIQUE: It was a compliment.

MIDGE: Monique, I'm not stupid.

MONIQUE: It was a shock. Charlie was happily married and suddenly it was all on the rocks.

MIDGE: His marriage had been snorrendous for years in case you hadn't noticed.

MONIQUE: They had their problems and you coming on the scene didn't help.

MIDGE: I didn't give your beloved son a second glance. He came chasing me!

MONIQUE: You didn't encourage him in the slightest?

MIDGE: No! I wasn't looking for marriage, I wasn't ready for marriage but much to my surprise I totally fell for him. I didn't mean to but I did! Now if you want to keep pushing the logline 'she used her assets to get his,' then I swear to you, Lady M, you'll get as good as you give!

MONIQUE: I certainly couldn't accuse you of not being forthright.

MIDGE: We're obviously never going to become besties for our resties, but we don't need to turn this into the Middle East. It's your choice.

MONIQUE: This is a very special day for me. All I ask is you respect that.

MIDGE: Then you respect me!

The tension is cut by the entry of LIAM, *42, and his wife* CHRISSY, *40.* LIAM *is a big forceful man with a perpetual half-frown on his face. The warrior ever prepared for battle. By contrast his wife* CHRISSY *appears tense and contained with a forced half-smile on her face. She hates these gatherings and has an undertow of anger towards most of the others and* MONIQUE *in particular that she tries to suppress.* MONIQUE *beams and moves across and hugs* LIAM *and kisses* CHRISSY *on the cheek.*

MONIQUE: Chrissy, Liam, lovely to see you both.

LIAM: I need a drink. I've had a shit of a week.

He heads for the silver ice bucket and pours himself a generous champagne which disappears in two gulps. He pours himself another. CHARLIE *reappears and the two brothers greet each other with a decidedly half-hearted high-five as they both head back to join the conversation.*

CHRISSY: Place is looking great, Monique.

MONIQUE: I do try and do it justice.

CHRISSY: [*peering out through the window*] And the garden. Beautiful.

MONIQUE: I have a very good hedge man. Not so great on lawns but excellent with the shrubs and hedges.

CHRISSY: Hi, Midge.

MIDGE: [*without enthusiasm*] Hi, Chrissy.

CHRISSY: Like your dress. Not something I could wear these days but looks good on you.

LIAM: Why couldn't you wear it?

CHRISSY: I'm past the age where I feel the need to …

MIDGE: To what?

CHRISSY: Get men hot and bothered.

MIDGE: Sorry. Would you like me to go borrow my sister's Laura Ashley?

CHRISSY: If you've got it, flaunt it.

LIAM: Chrissy, there's nothing wrong with the way you look. If you did dress a little more adventurously, you'd still turn men's heads.

CHRISSY: I've got two lovers already. That's all I can cope with.

MONIQUE *looks at her sharply.*

Just joking. I did dream I was in bed with Jim Chalmers last week but all that happened was that he told me he knew I was doing it tough.

CHARLIE: So how are you doing running our state, Liam?

LIAM: Cut the sarcasm.

CHARLIE: You are a minister of the crown.

LIAM: For local government? My desk lamp has more power than I do. All I get to hear is whining NIMBY councillors blocking any attempt at getting a little medium density development near the CBD, or the neanderthal Nats on a holy crusade to make sure the last remaining tree in the state is felled by 2030.

CHARLIE: Get out of politics if it's that frustrating.

LIAM: I don't intend to be a junior minister for ever. If it's human to err, then our idiot Premier is more human than any of us.

CHARLIE: Tomorrow belongs to you?

LIAM: I'm going for the leadership. Or more correctly the leadership is coming after me. The numbers are being counted.

MONIQUE: That's wonderful, darling. You'd be so much better than Goofy Graham. When is it going to happen?

LIAM: We'll probably hold off until he loses the next election.

CHARLIE: Quite a way off then?

LIAM: Go too soon and you get called disloyal.

CHARLIE: Which of course you're not.

LIAM: [*annoyed*] He's an idiot! Everyone in the party knows he has to go.

> *There's an awkward silence broken by the arrival of* DANIEL *and* JUDY. DANIEL *42, the non-identical twin of* LIAM, *has an air of aloofness, as if this gathering is the last thing he wants to be at which could well be true, but his wife* JUDY, *41, has the glint of a warrior in her eye. She's fought battles with* MONIQUE *before and is ever prepared to recommence hostilities.* DANIEL *is inventively, if not a little bizarrely, dressed to signal that he's no suburban conformist, and* JUDY *is in a neat suit.*

MONIQUE: Daniel, Judy. How lovely to see you.

> *There are awkward welcoming embraces and a moment of silence.* DANIEL *nods to his two brothers and they return the favour perfunctorily and* JUDY *smiles at the two other wives.*

My three boys and their partners. How proud of you all I am, and how wonderful to have you all here on this very special day. The food is all laid out for you on the table. Just relax, drink champagne, graze and enjoy each other's company. As usual I'll say a few words a little later to try and express the happiness I always feel when we're all together, and with your indulgence, I'll sing my usual little musical offering later in the afternoon.

> *They all shuffle and look at each other and are led into a fairly tepid round of applause by* CHARLIE *who claps with more enthusiasm than the rest.*

CHARLIE: Looking forward to it, Mum.

MONIQUE: The years have taken their toll of my voice but hopefully there's still something of the old magic.

CHARLIE: I'm sure there will be.

MONIQUE: Relax and have a wander out in the garden. It's a lovely afternoon and there are deckchairs set up under shade.

They all gravitate towards the garden offstage with glasses of champagne in their hands. All except LIAM *who is checking messages on his iPhone and* MIDGE *who is about to go out but sees* LIAM *and doubles back. He looks up.*

MIDGE: I saw you on television last week.

LIAM: Ah, what was I talking about?

MIDGE: Can't remember but whoever did your make-up didn't know what the fuck they were doing.

LIAM: Really, did I look bad?

MIDGE: Shiny, sweaty and pink. And your hair was super-sad.

LIAM: That bad?

MIDGE: Get yourself a stylist or no-one under seventy's going to vote for you. Are you really going to run for Premier?

LIAM: Yes. Did I really look that bad?

MIDGE: Easily fixed. Here's my card.

She hands him her card.

Charlie thinks you haven't got a hope in hell, but if you had your own personal make-up specialist it'd make a big difference.

LIAM: [*eyes narrowing*] Charlie told you that? That I didn't have a hope in hell?

MIDGE: But hey, he thought that Trump could never make it.

LIAM: I'm not exactly like Trump.

MIDGE *nods.*

MIDGE: Your hair's bad but easily fixed.

MIDGE *considers.*

Well not that easy but, yeah … I could help.

CHARLIE *comes in from the garden looking for* MIDGE.

LIAM: Midge tells me you don't think I'll get to be Premier? Would you like to tell me why?

CHARLIE: We'll talk about it sometime but not now.

LIAM: I'd like to know now.

CHARLIE: It was just an opinion. I might be wrong.

LIAM: Why exactly do you hold that opinion?

CHARLIE: Not now, not today.

> *But of course* LIAM *won't forget it and glares at his younger brother then moves out into the garden.* CHARLIE *turns to* MIDGE.

Why did you tell him that?

MIDGE: Because it's true.

CHARLIE: Getting through this ordeal is hard enough without you throwing hand grenades.

> MONIQUE *comes in from the garden.*

MONIQUE: Charlie, Midge. Come out in the garden.

MIDGE: It's skin-kill ultraviolet out there.

MONIQUE: There's plenty of shade.

> MIDGE *points to her hair.*

MIDGE: Too much wind. I've just spent a fortune getting my hair done and it'll get blown to pieces.

MONIQUE: It's only a breeze.

MIDGE: There are gusts.

> MONIQUE *shrugs, fills her glass to the brim, exchanges a knowing look with* CHARLIE *which* MIDGE *notes and moves across to the far side of the room and sits with a grumpy look on her face.* CHARLIE *ushers* MONIQUE *out of her earshot.*

CHARLIE: Mum.

MONIQUE: What?

CHARLIE: Go easy on the champagne.

MONIQUE: Charlie! Don't be such a drag.

CHARLIE: Remember last year?

MONIQUE: [*indignant*] That was my fault? My fault! What are you saying. Judy was rude to me.

CHARLIE: Mum.

MONIQUE: She was deliberately rude. And if she tries it again this year she'll get more of the same.

CHARLIE: Yes, but—

MONIQUE: Frankly all three of you haven't distinguished yourself in your choice of wives, and when any of them cross the line in my house they'll get as good as they give and more.

CHARLIE: [*pointing to her full glass*] Please, Mum. Not too much.

> MONIQUE *gives him a withering look and moves out into the garden.* CHARLIE *moves across to* MIDGE*, exasperated.*

So what are you going to do? Sit inside all afternoon?

MIDGE: This hair cost me three hundred and fifty dollars.

CHARLIE: Three hundred and fifty?

MIDGE: I went to Jacques. If you want the best you have to pay for the best! I did it to pass muster with your dragon of a mother!

CHARLIE: It's only a light breeze out there.

MIDGE: There are GUSTS! Gusts! The trees are bending. I'm not blind.

CHARLIE: So what do I do for the rest of the afternoon. Sit here with you?

MIDGE: You spend next to no time with me in any case, so why change now?

CHARLIE: What?

MIDGE: The ski lodge! You left me sitting there for hours while you were off schussing down slopes or whatever it is you do.

CHARLIE: You told me you could ski.

MIDGE: You didn't tell me your friends were Olympic skiers.

CHARLIE: Celia tried out for the winter Olympics years ago.

MIDGE: When I did try she was grinning all over her stupid face.

CHARLIE: I offered to arrange lessons.

MIDGE: I can ski! Just not like a bloody Olympian!

CHARLIE: One stumble and you go back to the lodge for the rest of the stay.

MIDGE: I wasn't going to look like a goose. Maybe you could've understood that and come and talked to me about it. But of course you didn't. I don't know why you wanted to get married if the only time you ever intended to spend with me was in bed!

CHARLIE: We go out together all the time?

MIDGE: And you dump me and leave me stranded like the bloody yacht-club lunch? Off downstairs to watch cricket with your yachting mates and I'm left with that overweight bore.

CHARLIE: You seemed to be having a good conversation with him.

MIDGE: He was hitting on me. And you walk off and leave me. To watch cricket? Where if you're lucky something happens every second day?

CHARLIE: Bernie? Hitting on you?

MIDGE: Unless putting your hand near a woman's crotch is yachtie shorthand for 'let loose the spinnaker', then yes!

CHARLIE: Bernie? He's our president.

MIDGE: He's also a hands-everywhere predalingus who thinks he's irresistible because he owns one of those gross maxi-yachts. I don't get why you want to do that stupid Sydney to Hobart thing in the first place. You all freeze, get seasick and nearly drown.

CHARLIE: It's a huge sense of achievement when you make it.

MIDGE: You told me it's hellish!

CHARLIE: Midge, I'm on a boat with fifteen of the most influential men in the country. Most of my major accounts have come from them or been referrals from them.

MIDGE: So you do it just to drum up business.

CHARLIE: Advertising is the most cut-throat industry in the world. It's all about connections. And they're all good guys.

MIDGE: They're arrogant, smug, sexist and condescending. As soon as they hear I'm a beautician their eyes roll.

CHARLIE: You're imagining it.

MIDGE: It took me over two years to qualify. It wasn't easy.

CHARLIE: I know.

MIDGE: Three of my year failed. Mind you two of those were brickheads.

Beat.

And I don't want to go to Perth with that other condescending couple either.

CHARLIE: Colin and Harriet? They're lovely.

MIDGE: Harriet.

CHARLIE: What's wrong with Harriet?

MIDGE: Nothing apart from the fact that it's bloody obvious to everyone except her noodlebrained husband that the thing she'd like to do most in life is to jump into bed with you—

CHARLIE: That's ridiculous!

MIDGE: All those little arm strokes? Batting of eyelids.

She demonstrates Harriet's habits.

Giggling at everything you say? Most of which isn't the slightest bit funny.

CHARLIE: You're being stupid.

MIDGE: I'm not blind. And why are we going to Margaret River? Five and a half hour flight? To see bloody Fleetwood Mac. Fleetwood Mac? Who in God's name ever listens to Fleetwood Mac these days?

CHARLIE: Certainly not your airheaded friends. The 'Okedoke' Brothers? The 'Deedle-Deedle-Dees'? Do they honestly think that's music?

MIDGE: Yes! And played by guys our own age. Not an ageing fun-sponge like I've got.

CHARLIE: Okay. So you're going to sit here all afternoon?

CHRISSY comes in with an empty glass and heads for the champagne ice bucket. She smiles and nods at CHARLIE and MIDGE, noting the tension between them.

MIDGE: [*to* CHARLIE] You go and enjoy yourself.

CHARLIE looks at her, shakes his head and goes. CHRISSY looks at MIDGE.

CHRISSY: Problems?

MIDGE: I may as well not be married to him.

CHRISSY: Really.

MIDGE: Shows me off to all his friends at the wedding and then I hardly see him. If he's not spending ridiculous hours working out how to get people to buy more chocolate bars, shampoo, vitamins or whatever, he's off with the boys surfing, yachting, playing tennis, or watching any form of sport that he can get on a screen. I caught him watching lawn bowls one day! Eighty-year-olds who could hardly lift the bloody things!

CHRISSY: Liam is never off the iPhone plotting the downfall of our Premier.

MIDGE: Why do we put up with them?

CHRISSY: As far as I can remember he probably fathered my four kids and I'm not about to become a penniless single mother.

MIDGE: I want kids.

CHRISSY: Don't. You might get little monsters like mine.

MIDGE: Charlie swore he wanted them until after we tied the knot then suddenly he'd 'reconsidered'.

CHRISSY: Reconsidered?

MIDGE: He'd been through all the 'up all nights' and nappy-changing and couldn't face it again.

CHRISSY: I doubt if Charlie ever got up in the nights or changed nappies. Penny would have done it all.

MIDGE: Yeah.

CHRISSY: Charlie is all about Charlie.

MIDGE: So I'm finding out.

CHRISSY: Nice guy. Not a killer like mine, but all about himself nonetheless.

MIDGE: I'm bloody near clinically deeped at the moment.

CHRISSY: Deeped?

MIDGE: Depressed. It's not just Charlie. This bunkass client called Carla, from Bellevue Hill, dripping jewellery. Always comes in with a photo of a new hairstyle she wants and then hates it. Well this one was Jesus awful to start with and on top of that I fucked it up and she screamed at me and I did the full poody. Told her take her broomstick and fly away and I was sacked on the spot. So no job, no references and all Charlie can think of is that I do 'my bad' humble pie and belly grovel to the old gorgon. According to Charlie it's all my fault.

CHRISSY *nods.*

CHRISSY: It's always our fault.

MIDGE *nods.*

MIDGE: Broomstick was maybe pushing it. But hey. Enough of dark side. You've got a husband on his way to be Premier?

CHRISSY: Yeah, and I'm supposed to devote myself totally to the cause. And also single-handedly raise four feral kids whose names he can hardly remember.

MIDGE: Doesn't sound like hacky-sacky fun times.

CHRISSY: Always expecting me to cook meals for his political allies and they're all thugs like him and the whole night is non-stop character assassination and none of them even register what they're eating so I finally said no.

MIDGE: Good for you.

CHRISSY: Not so good. He spends the next week screaming that don't I realise that this is a crucial moment in his career and how important it is that we work as a team, et cetera, et cetera, rant rant. So I say okay they can come and I serve them reheated meat pies and apple pies for dessert.

MIDGE: They got the message.

CHRISSY: No. They're such slobs they loved it.

She gets up.

I'm sure you'll get another job. Better go and see what's going on.

MIDGE: [*gloomy*] Hope so.

CHARLIE *comes in from the garden looking cross.*

CHARLIE: Midge, bloody hell! You can't sit here alone for the rest of the afternoon.

He sighs and sits down beside her.

I've just been on the phone to your boss.

MIDGE: Cheryl?

CHARLIE: She's calmed down and she says she knows Carla is an impossible old horror and that you're great at what you do and she wants you back.

MIDGE *stares at him.*

MIDGE: She really said that?

CHARLIE: Yeah.

MIDGE: She really said I was great at my job?

CHARLIE: Sort of.

Beat.

She just wants you to write a few words to Carla to say you did make a mistake—

MIDGE: No.

CHARLIE: [*getting up*] Okay, I tried.

MIDGE: All right. I'll write a note. But I won't do tummy time.

CHARLIE: Just courteous. Admit you were wrong. I'll draft it for you. In English.

MIDGE: Okay, but don't turn me into Gertie the Goomba.

CHARLIE: Courteous, dignified. Okay?

> MIDGE *stands.*

MIDGE: Thanks.

> CHARLIE *nods.*

CHARLIE: Come outside.

> MIDGE *shrugs.*

MIDGE: Okay, if you're happy to see three hundred and fifty dollars of hairstyling gone with the wind.

> *She gives* CHARLIE *a kiss on the cheek.*

Thanks.

> *They go outside. Almost immediately* MONIQUE *comes in heading for the champagne.* CHARLIE *momentarily comes back inside to warn his mother against excessive drinking but thinks better of it. What will be will be. He shakes his head and goes out again just as* JUDY *enters with a glint in her eye. It is obvious she's followed* MONIQUE *in.* MONIQUE *turns and anticipates what's to come and composes herself.*

MONIQUE: Hello, Judy. Quite lovely out there in the garden, isn't it?

JUDY: Yes it is. Monique, this is a special day for you and I wasn't going to do anything to make it any less special, but after what happened last week I feel I have to say something.

MONIQUE: [*calm, innocent*] What happened last week?

JUDY: It's good that you have lunches with Daniel, but—

MONIQUE: He's my son.

JUDY: But I don't appreciate it when you use those lunches to undermine me.

MONIQUE: I'm not sure I understand what you're talking about?

JUDY: How we educate our daughter is a matter for us.

MONIQUE: Of course.

JUDY: You apparently told Daniel it was disgraceful that we're taking Lisa out of her private school and sending her to a state school.

MONIQUE: I did express surprise. She's at the best school in Sydney. Is it financial?

JUDY: No, it's not financial. We don't like her group of friends or how she's behaving.

MONIQUE: Her friends come from some of the best homes in Sydney.

JUDY: They're awful little snobs with awful values.

MONIQUE: Awful values?

JUDY: My daughter impersonated a perfectly decent girl online and made her appear to be a promiscuous slut.

MONIQUE: I'm sure she didn't.

JUDY: Oh yes she did. And the girl was then viciously and anonymously slut-shamed online, and my daughter and her friends all thought it was hilarious.

MONIQUE: I'm sure Lisa would never do anything like that.

JUDY: She confessed. But only when the proof was overwhelming.

MONIQUE: Young girls always have lapses.

JUDY: That's not just a lapse, Monique. It's totally unacceptable.

MONIQUE: But to blame the school?

JUDY: I do. I'm taking her out of there and I didn't appreciate you telling Daniel I was sabotaging my daughter's future.

MONIQUE: But for heaven's sake. Sending her to Concord High? Concord?

JUDY: Concord High's academic results are actually better than the school we pay thirty-eight thousand dollars a year to turn our daughter into a heartless little sociopath.

MONIQUE: Judy, I know you came from a struggling family and went to state school yourself and did very very well, which is a credit to you—

JUDY: Not in your eyes.

MONIQUE: What are you talking about?

JUDY: When I first started dating Daniel you took him aside and said it might help my career if I had some elocution lessons.

MONIQUE: I was trying to help.

JUDY: Despite my grating vowels, I have survived quite well.

MONIQUE: You've done amazingly well but I wish you'd get that chip off your shoulder—

JUDY: Chip?

MONIQUE: That perverse superiority of someone from the wrong side of the tracks who happens to make it. Yes, I told Daniel that I thought you were doing Lisa a great disservice by taking her out of that fine school—

JUDY: Fine school?

MONIQUE: Okay, she's possibly mixing with the wrong group of girls but—

JUDY: All those girls are the same. They're taught to judge people by the size of their waterside mansions, their designer clothes, their expensive cars or huge boats.

MONIQUE: That's nonsense. They're children of parents who live well but also appreciate opera, ballet, theatre, the fine arts. Parents with power and influence. Taking Lisa out of that school will be depriving her of connections that will be invaluable right through her life. Do you really think it's going to help her to mix with the children of plumbers and car salesmen and suburban accountants.

JUDY: Monique, you are such an appalling snob.

JUDY *turns to walk away in disgust.* MONIQUE *is furious.*

MONIQUE: Whether you realise it or not, there is a social hierarchy, and if you're part of its top echelons it gives access to a life of elegance and ease and the satisfaction of knowing that you count. And you're ripping your daughter away from the possibility of ever enjoying all that. And why? Because you've never gotten over your hatred of the people who are fortunate enough to live that life. Your envy has turned us into the enemy. Don't deny your daughter her birthright.

JUDY: If Lisa goes to a state school her career will be crippled through lack of the right contacts, and her cultural horizons will be limited to karaoke nights and drag-car races? Is that what I'm hearing?

JUDY *turns to walk away then turns and launches vehemently again.*

The real reason you hate the thought of your granddaughter going to a state school is that you don't want to suffer the stigma when your friends to find out. Well tough luck, Monique. You're going to have to live with that humiliating disgrace.

JUDY turns to leave. DANIEL *comes inside looking for her. He sizes up the situation and sees that his mother's eyes are flashing fire.*

DANIEL: What's going on?

MONIQUE: Your wife is just so rude. So graceless and rude.

She leaves. DANIEL *turns to* JUDY, *exasperated.*

DANIEL: Do you have to pick a fight with her every time we come here?

JUDY: I won't have her interfering with how we bring up our daughter.

DANIEL: We? Since when did I have a say in it?

JUDY: You seem to side with her at every bloody turn.

DANIEL: Just be a little bit sensitive, can't you?

JUDY: Sensitive? When is she ever sensitive?

DANIEL: It's her old school. I've never seen her happier than when Lisa was admitted there.

JUDY: Probably only because of the large contributions she kept making to the school's building fund.

DANIEL: Come on!

JUDY: Well it certainly wasn't our daughter's academic record.

DANIEL: You've always had it in for that school.

JUDY: The building fund? What more was there to build? They have a concert hall, two assembly halls, three basketball courts, an Olympic swimming pool, three sports ovals, five grass tennis courts, a squash court, a state-of-the-art science centre and a wellness centre— what's next? A velodrome and helipad?

DANIEL: She didn't donate to the building fund. It was the musical instrument acquisition fund.

JUDY: Half the violin section are no doubt playing Stradivariuses already.

DANIEL: Judy—

JUDY: The old girls of that school only ever associate with other old girls for the rest of their lives. I want our daughter to associate with a wider spectrum of humanity than that.

DANIEL: Like we do? Name one friend of ours that doesn't live in a multimillion-dollar house?

JUDY: Yes, but our friends are left of centre.

DANIEL: A few of them vote Labor which is now somewhere to the right of where the Liberal Party used to be under John Howard.

JUDY: That's not true.

DANIEL: When I told your dear friends Marcia and Neville that I'd been voting Greens for the last thirty years, he exploded and asked if I wanted the country to return to the Stone Age.

JUDY: Well, yes, Neville …

She shakes her head. Neville is a pain.

But the fact remains that Lisa's school is totally out of touch with contemporary reality. Their houses are Blaxland, Wentworth, Lawson and Bell. Apart from them all being male in a girls' school, they were the explorers who found a path through the Blue Mountains and thereby ensured the destruction of First Nations culture.

DANIEL: Must you be so bloody woke! Okay, it's a school stacked with little snobs but try and be a little sensitive to how important its been to Mum's life. She was head prefect.

JUDY: God help those poor little girls whose hats weren't straight. They're probably still under psychiatric care.

DANIEL: Stop it! She's not that bad!

JUDY: Oh yes she is.

DANIEL: Look, I do agree that Concord High is probably a good option for our daughter given what's happened but let's just do it without throwing it in Mum's face.

JUDY: So now you've changed your tune. Concord High is okay now. Not what you said when you came home from lunch with her.

DANIEL: Okay, I can see both sides! She would make social connections that would help her in life if she stays where she is.

JUDY: What are you, Daniel? A Greens-voting social snob!

DANIEL: And what are you? A cruise missile aimed at anyone who hasn't survived the school of hard knocks!

JUDY: If I'm so horrible, divorce me!

DANIEL: It's not something I'm contemplating.

JUDY: Well, I am!

DANIEL: Divorce? Are you serious?

JUDY: If you just stood up to her occasionally.

DANIEL: It's not me you're divorcing, it's my mother?

JUDY: It's a pretty good reason.

> *She goes out to the garden.* DANIEL *stands there.* MONIQUE, *who has obviously observed Judy leave, enters.*

MONIQUE: Did you put your foot down?

DANIEL: Mum—

MONIQUE: Taking her out of the best school in Australia and dumping her in an under-resourced state school is insane.

DANIEL: What Lisa did wasn't nice.

MONIQUE: All girls can get a little nasty at that age. She'll be fine.

DANIEL: Mum, what Lisa did was pretty horrible. And it's not just that.

MONIQUE: What else is it?

DANIEL: I was walking down the street with her the other day and some girls passed us dressed differently to her, and with total contempt in her voice she said 'Westies'!

MONIQUE: Oh for God's sake. There are class divisions in any society. Always will be. If you were in India, would you rather be born a Brahmin or an untouchable?

DANIEL: This is Australia!

MONIQUE: And you still think you live in a classless society? Get real. If you're happy that you're ensuring your daughter's cultural horizons are limited to *Keeping Up with the Kardashians*, then fine.

DANIEL: That's exactly what her friends watch now.

MONIQUE: Take your wife's side as usual. Would you dare do otherwise?

DANIEL: Mum, she has a point, you have a point.

MONIQUE: But hers are the only points you listen to.

DANIEL: Look, to be totally honest, I do think it's a pity she'll be leaving a school with a teaching staff and facilities as good as she has now, but if I make a huge issue out of this …

MONIQUE: What? What will happen?

DANIEL: She's threatened …

MONIQUE: Divorce?

DANIEL: Yes.

MONIQUE: Good. You deserve someone who doesn't go through life with a chip on her shoulder. Honestly, haven't you had just about enough?

DANIEL: Sometimes I do get depressed. Judy's pigheadedness can get me down.

MONIQUE: She's a unmitigated bully. You'd be better off without her. You're sure to find someone else who's much better for you.

DANIEL: Just like that?

MONIQUE: Of course you will.

DANIEL: I get tongue-tied whenever an attractive woman comes within ten metres of me. And I'm not exactly a wonderful catch. Financially.

MONIQUE: Whose fault is that? You should've taken a few more years and qualified as an architect. Not stayed a—what is it you are?

DANIEL: An architectural draftsman.

MONIQUE: If you separate from Judy I'll fund you to do architecture.

DANIEL *stares at her.*

I mean it. I want you to enjoy some happiness in life which you'll never do with her.

DANIEL: You're bribing me to end my marriage?

MONIQUE: Not a bribe, an incentive.

[*Off his reaction*] You've just admitted you've thought seriously about it yourself.

DANIEL: I don't want to do architecture.

MONIQUE: You're happy to stay what you are?

DANIEL: No. But if I did anything it'd be structural engineering.

MONIQUE: [*horrified*] Engineering? Where's the artistry in that?

DANIEL: Engineers design most of our big buildings in any case. Architects just do a bit of tarting up. And maths was by far my best subject at school.

MONIQUE: Okay, if you must, I'll fund that.

DANIEL: Serious?

MONIQUE: Of course.

DANIEL: But only if I divorce Judy?

MONIQUE: Do you want to stay married to her? Honestly?

DANIEL *sighs.*

DANIEL: Big step.

MONIQUE: Is there still electricity? In the bedroom?

DANIEL: That fades in any marriage.

MONIQUE: If it's faded totally, the marriage is over.

DANIEL: It hasn't faded … totally.

MONIQUE: That's not sounding like a hot cot to me.

DANIEL: She's a partner in a top law firm. She works very hard.

MONIQUE: Not tonight, Josephine? That's what I'm hearing?

DANIEL: It's not that bad.

MONIQUE: The spark has gone. That's what I'm hearing in your voice. The spark has gone.

DANIEL: [*irritated*] It's not the only important thing in a marriage. After Dad died, you didn't feel life was over.

MONIQUE: It wasn't. Believe me.

DANIEL: What? You … ?

MONIQUE: What did you expect me to do? Join a religious order?

DANIEL: I never saw you with anyone else. None of us did.

> MONIQUE *continues to look evasive.*

The only other guy we ever saw at the house was Uncle Alan—

> *He stares at her.*

You had an affair with your sister's husband?

MONIQUE: She's never found out.

DANIEL: It's still going on?

MONIQUE: Oh for God's sake. She doesn't know a thing!

DANIEL: This has been happening for all these years?

MONIQUE: If she doesn't give him enough of what he needs it's her damn fault.

DANIEL: All those times he comes to fix things?

MONIQUE: He does fix things.

DANIEL: A little more than the light bulbs it seems.

MONIQUE: I'm normal with normal needs. Why the shock?

DANIEL: He isn't exactly your type, is he?

MONIQUE: What's my type?

DANIEL: I doubt he's ever seen an opera or listened to Mahler. Look, don't get me wrong. But … a panel beater?

MONIQUE: A very successful panel beater. He employs thirty men. And only does upmarket European models.

DANIEL: He had a very earthy turn of phrase and I doubt he'd been to many operas.

MONIQUE: The more opera a man listens to, the worse he is in bed. Your Uncle Alan at least knows which end is up.

DANIEL: [*sudden thought*] He was around a lot even *before* Dad died.

MONIQUE: So?

DANIEL: You always rabbited on about how Dad was the love of your life and no-one could ever replace him.

MONIQUE: He was a darling. But your Uncle Alan was much better in bed, which was a bloody relief.

DANIEL *watches as his mother goes to fill her glass.*

DANIEL: Mum! No more champagne.

MONIQUE: Oh, tosh to you! And I meant what I said. Ditch that witch of a wife of yours and I'll finance whatever degree you want to get. It's time you had a better deal in life.

DANIEL *looks thoughtful and moves out into the garden.* CHRISSY *comes in to get a champagne refill.* MONIQUE *eyes her narrowly.*

MONIQUE: I'm still waiting.

CHRISSY: For what, Monique?

MONIQUE: For that invitation.

[*Off* CHRISSY'*s blank reaction*] You were going to invite me to see your remodelled kitchen.

CHRISSY: Oh … really?

MONIQUE: And it would be nice to reacquaint myself with my four grandchildren.

CHRISSY: I'm sorry, but I absolutely can't remember asking you.

MONIQUE: Really.

She takes out her iPhone and scrolls down.

Here's the text message.

CHRISSY: [*reading*] Oh yes. That's right. Sorry. I'll work out a date and call you.

MONIQUE: Perhaps we could work out a date now?

CHRISSY: I haven't got my diary. I'm sorry, but the family and Liam's career make my life very frenetic.

MONIQUE: [*pointing to her screen*] This was the third time you've promised to invite me, by the way.

CHRISSY: Monique, life is more hectic than you can imagine. Sally gets hit by every bug that goes around. I've had to race her to emergency twice in the last month and and I've been diagnosed with osteoarthritis in the right elbow and it's possible I'll need a knee replacement—

MONIQUE: If you don't ever really intend to invite me, just say so.

CHRISSY: Monique, that's not what I—

MONIQUE: Then I could learn to live with the occasional shots of my grandchildren Liam sends on his phone.

CHRISSY: Of course we'll have you over.

MONIQUE: That would really, really be nice.

> MONIQUE *goes out into the garden, leaving* CHRISSY *visibly distressed.* LIAM *enters and frowns.*

LIAM: What's wrong?

CHRISSY: Your mother's been at me again.

LIAM: About what?

CHRISSY: Why I don't invite her over.

LIAM: Why don't you?

CHRISSY: [*bursting out*] When would I ever have time! If it's not the kids, it's you suddenly telling me you're arriving with four of your political mates for dinner.

LIAM: Occasionally.

CHRISSY: More than occasionally.

LIAM: If we go to a restaurant, everyone overhears.

CHRISSY: Overhears what? You plotting the downfall of the guy you're supposed to be all totally and solidly loyal to.

LIAM: He's not up to the job.

CHRISSY: Then why not say so. Every time you're ever asked if there's a leadership battle going on you say everyone in the party is a hundred percent behind him.

LIAM: We don't want to warn him about when the move is coming.

CHRISSY: He knows it's coming?

LIAM: Of course.

> [*Gleam in his eye*] But he doesn't know when.

CHRISSY: Neither do you and your mates.

LIAM: Certain things have got to fall into place.

CHRISSY: Like getting the numbers, which it's obvious you haven't got.

LIAM: How do you know that?

CHRISSY: I'm not deaf.

LIAM: It's taking a while for the party to realise what an electoral disaster the fuckwit is going to prove.

CHRISSY: From what I heard the last time they came, your numbers man seems to think you're still twenty votes short.

LIAM: Eighteen. Eighteen short.

CHRISSY: So how many more of these plotters soirées do I have to endure?

LIAM: You're sitting down with some of the sharpest minds in the state.

CHRISSY: Then God help us.

LIAM: Honey, is there anything you're happy about in life? Anything? Being married to you is like being married to an encyclopedia of medical and mental disorders.

CHRISSY: Mental?

LIAM: The migraines, the anxiety attacks, the sleepless nights, the depressive episodes—

CHRISSY: Between you, four uncontrollable kids you hardly see and your bloody mother, it's a wonder I'm not in a bloody asylum!

She goes outside. DANIEL *enters.*

DANIEL: There you are.

LIAM: What's up?

DANIEL: Mum's drinking too much.

LIAM: What's new.

DANIEL: Picking fights with our wives.

LIAM: What do you want me to do about it?

DANIEL: Don't let her drink any more before her speech because that's when she really unloads.

LIAM: Why don't we all just go home.

DANIEL: This is her big moment of the year. Bail out of this and it would kill her.

LIAM: Not likely. She's as tough as old boots.

DANIEL: Underneath that imperious surface she's very vulnerable.

LIAM: No way.

DANIEL: And if we get through the speech there's still the aria.

LIAM: Bejesus yes. Isn't it time to tell her to stop?

DANIEL: That really would kill her. The delusion she was on her way to being the next Maria Callas has kept her life afloat.

LIAM: And sunk ours. Do you think she really believes it?

DANIEL: Dead set.

LIAM: She was good enough to get into the Conservatorium.

DANIEL: No.

LIAM: No?

DANIEL: Judy researched it. She failed her audition three years in a row.

LIAM: Oh shit!

DANIEL: Judy finally got fed up with her pretensions and searched out one of the retired teachers. She had talent but not enough. They only take the best of the best.

LIAM: Oh my God. Judy's not going to spring that one, is she?

DANIEL: No, she just needed to know for her own satisfaction.

LIAM: Jesus. The old fake.

Beat.

I just don't get people who delude themselves.

DANIEL: Really?

LIAM: [*glaring at him*] I *am* going to be Premier of this state, Daniel. And sooner than you think.

DANIEL: Okay. Fine.

LIAM: We do focus groups, and I come out as decisive, forceful, capable.

DANIEL: Okay.

LIAM: At least I have ambition. Where exactly is your life going, Daniel? Charlie, to his credit, has done better than I ever would have expected but where is your life going?

DANIEL: Where is it supposed to be going?

LIAM: What do you earn? Seventy K a year?

DANIEL: A bit more.

LIAM: Now I might be a sexist prick but I couldn't stand to be married to a woman who earns what five, six times what I do?

DANIEL: Lay off.

LIAM: You could have done two more years and become an architect.

DANIEL: I don't want to become a fucking architect!

LIAM: I might be old-fashioned but I couldn't stand being in a marriage where I earned less than my wife.

DANIEL: You and I may be twins but I'm not you. And glad of it.

LIAM: Where's your pride, man?

DANIEL: Liam. Shut the fuck up and concentrate on getting through this unholy charade.

LIAM: Yeah, it is a charade.

DANIEL: More a charade than you imagine.

LIAM: What's that mean?

DANIEL *nods.*

DANIEL: According to Mum, she had most perfect marriage in the history of the world. To the most perfect man. Odd that Dad's mistress of twenty-five years turns up at his hospital bed when he's dying. Thank God I was the one who was there and not Mum.

LIAM: The irony is she worshipped Dad. Never looked at another man for the rest of her life.

DANIEL: Hah. That's part two of the grand charade.

LIAM: What is?

DANIEL: She was also cheating on him!

LIAM: No way! Who with?

DANIEL: Uncle Alan.

LIAM: Uncle Alan?!

DANIEL: Turns out he wasn't just pounding car panels.

LIAM: Uncle Alan!

MONIQUE *comes in and overhears. She's cross with* DANIEL.

MONIQUE: That was told to you in confidence.

LIAM: Uncle Alan!

MONIQUE: Get over it. He was a tiger between the sheets, which is more than I can say for your father. Not a word about this. They're all coming in for my speech.

CHARLIE *enters.*

CHARLIE: Mum.

MONIQUE: What?

CHARLIE: Just go easy.

LIAM: On our wives.

DANIEL: We have to live with them.

MONIQUE: I always praise them to high heavens. Much more than they deserve.

CHARLIE: Chrissy seems upset already.

LIAM: When isn't she?

MONIQUE: She's the original princess who complains about the pea under her mattress.

DANIEL: Judy's upset too.

MONIQUE: She's upset? She was so rude she almost had me in tears.

DANIEL: Just go easy on them.

MONIQUE: For God's sake. I'll heap them with praise. Lie through my teeth as usual. Sweetness and light. Don't worry.

CHARLIE: Promise?

MONIQUE: What happened to my three bold fearless sons? Pussy-whipped. All of you.

CHARLIE: Mum, please.

MONIQUE: I will be the very model of a modern mother-in-law. Truly, relax.

She heads for the champagne.

CHARLIE: Mum! No more?

MONIQUE: Will you stop it? I'm fine. If there's one person at this gathering that can handle drink, it's me. In the ski lodge where I met your father he ended up with me because I drank all my competitors under the table.

CHARLIE: A fairytale romance.

MONIQUE: More fairytale than any of yours.

The wives come in as MONIQUE *prepares herself.* JUDY *looks angry,* MIDGE *is sullen and* CHRISSY *looks anxious.*

Please all have a seat. Make yourselves comfortable. On this day I do like to say a few words to you all because it is a very very special day for me. What a wonderful coincidence that my youngest son Charlie was born three years to the day after my two very non-identical twin boys, Liam and Daniel. I only ever had to remember one birthday, not three. Happy birthday, my gorgeous boys. Now you've all heard the family history but for the benefit of young

Midge, the newest and very welcome member to our little family fold, I'll do a short recap.

She looks around them beaming.

All of us hope to meet Prince Charming and live happily ever after, but the fact is I did. Your late father Kevin turned out to be Prince Charming Plus. Well perhaps that's overegging it a little. He might never have been quite the life of the party and he did occasionally put his foot in it and leave me to do the damage control, and he wasn't exactly George Clooney to look at, but what a heart. What a heart. Okay, he did have the occasional outburst of temper and could be grumpy in the mornings but more often than not he was a sweetie who cared about others. Whenever we went abroad to poor countries he always went out with coins in his pockets to put in outstretched cups. Which did get us into trouble once in New York when a black man with an outstretched cup turned out to be drinking coffee and he got quite badly roughed up, but he was ever resilient. Ever resilient. 'It is what it is,' was his most frequent utterance and I felt the warm glow of his love my entire life.

She reflects.

Before we met I was a student at the Conservatorium on the verge of a singing career that my tutors were confident was going to take me to the pinnacle of the profession. La Scala, the Met, Covent Garden were all mentioned. Sure it was only a possibility but they were confident it was a real possibility. It was all so totally heady and exciting. But then … Kevin. I knew I had met the man I was going to spend my life with. But he was a brilliant mining engineer working in a remote mining community in WA. I had the choice. A possible, very possible brilliant career, or love. Finally, there was only one choice. Love.

She smiles at the memory.

And I'm not sorry. I hadn't misjudged him. Within twenty-five years, he had built a thriving international business and I found myself married to a very wealthy man. And mother of three wonderful boys. The thought of a world without those three in it fills me with horror. Thank God I made the choice I did. Even today, offer me a standing ovation at La Scala or my three beautiful boys and they'd win every time. Sadly, Kevin left us too early. But the gap left by Kevin was filled by my three amazing sons. What mother was ever so blessed. All of them successful, and as a huge bonus, all of them married to exceptional wives who have given me the gift of seven wonderful grandchildren.

She beams at her three sons in turn.

Please indulge me if, before I extol the virtues of my wonderful daughters-in-law, I spend a second or two on my brilliant boys. The twins. Liam born ten minutes before his brother and first off the mark ever since. Destined without doubt to lead this state to a bright future any time now. Capable, strong, decisive and I'm conceited enough to think that a lot of those strength genes came from me. Daniel. Not every male has to be strong and decisive. Daniel is my sensitive and artistic one. A hugely talented young pianist who could and should have been gracing concert stages around the world in the opinion of many. But like myself, love sometimes intervenes, and with love came marriage and children and a wife who had to be supported through the last years of an unfinished law degree. Choices had to be made and given what she's achieved since, I can totally see why Judy felt it was *her* career that had to come first.

MONIQUE *smiles sweetly at* JUDY *who is furious and is about to object but* DANIEL *manages to calm her down.*

And Charlie, ever-smiling Charlie. Charming, courteous, loved by all but with a business brain and a creative ability second to none. His advertising agency is now one of the most sought-after in the country and in terms of wealth, it has to be said, my youngest son has left his older brothers in his wake, which is not to say that aren't still both successes in their own fields, with I suspect more success to come in both cases.

She smiles at DANIEL, *referencing their secret pact, then turns her focus on the wives.*

And now my wonderful daughters-in-law. Judy. A woman, and I'm sure she won't mind me saying this, from anything but a privileged background. Sharing a tiny room with three sisters. Going cold in winter because her single mother couldn't pay the power bills but what a triumph. Partner in a big law firm. Amazing. Sometimes it has been said that her upbringing has left her with a chip on her shoulder, and some have called her tactless, but we all live with a legacy from our past.

MONIQUE *beams at* JUDY *who again is furious but* DANIEL *again calms her down.*

Chrissy. It isn't fashionable these days for many wives to concede that their husband's career comes first, but Chrissy does. And let's not pretend that's easy for her. I'm sure her children will turn out wonderfully in the long run but Chrissy won't mind me saying that her kind nature has perhaps hindered her from applying the discipline they need. High spirits are high spirits but frankly when their grandmother is good enough to babysit them and they lock her in the media room and I have to call my son on my phone to get me out, that's a red line for me. But as I said, I'm sure they'll be fine in the long run.

She patently isn't sure.

And Midge. Our newest. What a pretty young thing she is. And with such an inventive way of expressing herself. Who knows if she and Charlie have enough in common to last the distance but that's for the future to tell. It is a little sad for Grandmother here that until Charlie finally sorts things out with custody I don't get to see my two wonderful granddaughters. But as my late dear husband used to say quite frequently, 'It is what it is.' Thank you, all of you, being here with me on this special day and seeing you all here only makes me even surer of the wisdom of that the age-old saying 'There is no family without friction, but love is the oil that fixes everything.' So let's go out in the garden and enjoy the rest of the afternoon and a little later, with your indulgence, accompanied by my brilliant son Daniel on the piano, I'll try the most ambitious aria I've ever attempted. To remind myself and yourselves of what might have been, but finally harbouring no regrets that it didn't happen.

She sweeps up her three sons and ferries them out into the garden, beaming. The three daughters-in-law watch her go. They're all furious.

JUDY: [*indicating the garden*] That's it. I am not putting myself through this ever again. Even if it means the end of my marriage.

CHRISSY: Lucky you. I haven't got a high-paying career. I'm stuck with Liam and four kids.

JUDY: You're a qualified teacher.

CHRISSY: Judy, I'd love to get out of my marriage and feel like I was doing something useful, but I have four young kids.

JUDY: Are things that bad?

CHRISSY: Yes, but a big part of what makes it unbearable is her!

She indicates out in the garden.

Lunch every fortnight with her and Liam comes home with his ego stroked and full of grievances she's planted in him.

JUDY: Same. Those mother-son lunches. You look at your watch and know she's badmouthing you as fast as her thin, venomous lips can move.

MIDGE: She's a full-on bitch.

JUDY: Are you and Charlie good?

MIDGE: Not really. I didn't realise what a total boyo he was. Every opportunity he gets, he's off with his sailing mates, his surfing mates, his old university mates, his old football teammates, his tennis mates. More mates than a chess bloody master. Needs 'space', he tells me. I tell him I didn't marry 'space', I married him and I expect us to be man and wife. He's about to go down to Melbourne for a wake for some mate who's quit the oxygen habit, and he'll be away for four days.

CHRISSY: That's not great.

MIDGE: I'll knock it out of him, don't worry. I don't expect to be worshipped but I won't play second fiddle to any bloody one. And he knows it. He says I'm a prettier version of Jacqui Lambie.

CHRISSY: Good for you.

MIDGE*'s phone dings and she moves away from them to read the text message and intermittently sends texts until she rejoins them later.*

JUDY: [*to* CHRISSY] Have you considered ending the marriage?

CHRISSY: I've put in the hard yards to get him to be Premier. I'm not about to watch him marry some young bimbo who gets all the perks if he finally makes it.

She points out to the garden.

I could put up with him if it wasn't for Monique. She terrorises me.

JUDY: Don't let her.

CHRISSY: She was at me today about why I didn't have her for dinner. I don't want her for bloody dinner. I don't want her anywhere near our house. The minute she walks in the door she's making snide comments about my kids. No discipline. Got to be firm with them.

JUDY: Yeah. Ah—

CHRISSY: What? You think I don't discipline them enough?

JUDY: They do seem—

CHRISSY: [*suddenly very emotional*] They're fucking uncontrollable! Do you think I don't know that? Do you think I don't try and discipline them? They just defy me. Stare me down. Do what they want to do. I can't even get them to come to the table when dinner's ready. They stay in their rooms and text each other. And my bloody husband's never there to help. They put on an act when he's around and he thinks they're wonderful! He can barely remember their names!

JUDY: Look, I'm not the greatest at discipline myself but last time I was at your place I did notice—

CHRISSY: Yes you told me!

JUDY: Oh.

CHRISSY: When they ask for something I should say no, and stick to it. Yes, you told me. And I try. I try but when they ask for the twentieth time I get so I can't stand it any longer. I shouldn't give in but it's the only way I can stop their whining. And yes it reinforces their bad behaviour so they do it again and again. I know all that. I know all the theory but I can't put it in practice. Not with that lot! You've only got one! One! And it seems you have enough trouble with her. Try having four!

JUDY: I'm sorry, I shouldn't have—

CHRISSY: You know the thing that hurts, really hurts to the point of destroying me? They can all see how upset I am. They all know they've driven me right to the end of my tether AND THEY DON'T BLOODY WELL CARE! THEY DON'T GIVE A SHIT! How can human beings inflict so much pain and know they're doing it and not give a shit? After the million things I've done for them. How can that be? What kind of species are we?

She breaks down and starts sobbing quietly.

JUDY: [*comforting her*] They're kids, Chrissy. Totally egocentric and selfish. Kids always are and always will be. The adult brain isn't fully in place until we're twenty-five.

CHRISSY: With my bloody husband, try fifty-five!

MIDGE *comes back, still staring at her iPhone and looking very cross. She notices* CHRISSY *crying.*

MIDGE: Problem?

JUDY: Yeah.

MIDGE: So have I.

JUDY: What's wrong?

MIDGE: My friend Celeste texted. Left her front gate open and her cat got run over. It's a British Shorthair. Very expensive. She loved it to death. Talked about nothing else. So she's really really upset and texts me. And I tell her I understand. Totally. And tell her I'll come across later but she says that she needs me now and I try and explain that I can't just run out on my mother-in-law's big pachanga so she gets back to me with 'What kind of friend are you? Belinda just died!' So I get back to her and say 'Okay baby. I get that. I get how you must feel and I really really do. I loved Belinda too. I'll get there as soon as I can,' and she texts back, 'Forget it. I won't be home. I've gone to a real friend's place. A friend who really cares.' And of course she's full-on volcano girl by now and can't be reasoned with, but I try. I get back to her and say, 'Where are you baby I'll be there.' But she's obviously baseball bat by this stage because nothing comes back. Ten minutes. Nothing. She's ghosted me. Can you get that? Well, fuck her and fuck her bloody cat! I didn't want to go in any case because Charlie is taking me out to a zang restaurant tonight to celebrate the one-year anniversary of our marriage. If the fuckwit has remembered, which he usually doesn't. Never forgets a meeting with his mates, but me? Different story.

She notices CHRISSY *is still crying.*

Hey, you're not a happy bunny, are you? What's wrong?

CHRISSY: It's fine.

JUDY: Are you okay to go outside?

CHRISSY: Yeah I'm fine.

> *They go, more to get away from the self-obsessed chatter of* MIDGE *than anything else.* MIDGE *is back on her iPhone already.*

MIDGE: [*to iPhone*] Millie, is Celeste with you? Oh, she's a pepper bitch at the best of times but her cat got its call to heaven and it's a full-on hizzy-fizzle because I didn't do instant sob sister so she's cut me and run to some simp to help her wet the carpet. Yeah. Couldn't stand that bloody cat of hers in any case. Ugly fucking thing. Yeah, she slept with it on her pillow. Any rate, if she wants to play games, fuck her. Too high maintenance. Ciao, adios and macaca.

> *She looks up as* CHARLIE *comes in.*

CHARLIE: Judy said you're having some kind of drama. Cats?

MIDGE: Fucking Celeste. It's over. Forget it. She's DTM.

> [*Off* CHARLIE's *puzzled look*] Dead to me. Is my Lady Jayne straight?

> CHARLIE *takes a cursory look at her hair comb at the back of her head and nods.*

CHARLIE: Yeah it's fine.

> MIDGE *isn't happy with his assessment and whips out her mirror to check for herself.*

MIDGE: [*annoyed*] It's totally kerwonkety. Jesus, Charlie. Do you want me looking like a sheen queen?

CHARLIE: If I knew what that was I'd probably say no. Could you occasionally speak English?

> MIDGE *sighs.*

MIDGE: I married bloody Barney Rubble. Did you get us into Aria tonight?

CHARLIE: Yeah, but I couldn't get front table.

MIDGE: Well, sorry. I'm not going!

CHARLIE: It's one from the front.

MIDGE: If you're not at the window, you don't get the whole harbour view. Why do you always book so fucking late! It's like Hayman. We miss out on poolside because you booked too late.

CHARLIE: We cancel Hayman too?

MIDGE: Just try and get organised, will you?

CHARLIE: You really want me to cancel Aria?

MIDGE: Yes! I don't want to spend the whole meal looking at the backs of the people important enough to get a view. Try the Quay and if you can't get harbour view there, I guess bloody Ursula's.

She shakes her head.

I should've married Nick. He could call anywhere and get the best seats with just five minutes' notice.

She sweeps imperiously out. LIAM *comes in and sees* CHARLIE *shaking his head in despair.*

LIAM: You've made a rod for your own back there, bro.

CHARLIE: Yeah.

LIAM: How could you not see?

CHARLIE: Lay off!

LIAM: She might be ichywawa in the bedroom but couldn't you see she would make your life hell everywhere else? She's not just high maintenance, she's the original Miss Maserati.

CHARLIE: [*gloomy*] She actually wants me to buy her one.

LIAM: Couldn't you see it coming?

CHARLIE: I thought I could keep it in check.

LIAM: Mate, she would be harder to control than supermarket trolley with three bung wheels. So what are you going to do?

CHARLIE: What do you mean?

LIAM: Are you honestly going to go through the rest of your days shackled to her?

CHARLIE: Mate, my first wife is about to get half of everything I have. I can't afford to give away the next half.

LIAM: Your business is expanding right?

CHARLIE: Yeah, going gangbusters.

LIAM: In ten years' time, your net worth is going to be much bigger than it is now. Do it now and lose less.

CHARLIE: Hadn't thought of that.

LIAM: Why in the hell did you let Penny go? She's quality.

CHARLIE: She let me go.

LIAM: Because you couldn't keep it in your pants?

CHARLIE: Actually no.

LIAM: Then, what?

CHARLIE: The marriage was getting a little … stale.

LIAM: So?

CHARLIE: I suggested a little … maybe … swinging.

LIAM: Swinging?

CHARLIE: We tried and it was a disaster. She said it was the final straw in the coffin.

LIAM: You fucking idiot.

CHARLIE: Of course your marriage is just brilliant, isn't it?

LIAM: Chrissy is a drama queen.

CHARLIE: All her fault? Out there weeping her eyes out an it's all her fault.

LIAM: I give her everything she needs.

CHARLIE: Except ever being a father? She needs some help with that ravening wolfpack of kids of yours? She's at the end of her tether.

LIAM: You've been talking to her?

CHARLIE: I don't need to. I saw her walking out of here. She's a really nice person and you're turning her into a wreck.

DANIEL *comes in from the garden.*

DANIEL: You've got a pretty fragile wife out there, Liam.

LIAM: What is this? A fucking pile-on? If I became what she wanted me to be I'd have to give up my whole career.

DANIEL: Sounds like a good plan, bro.

LIAM: And become a nothing like you!

CHARLIE: God help us if we were all like you.

LIAM: And what's wrong with me, apart from the fact that I don't stay at home and mind the kids and cook the meals and all that shit?

CHARLIE: You're a druggie, mate, and your drug is power and you're totally addicted.

DANIEL: And it's turned you into a total shit.

CHARLIE: He was always a total shit.

LIAM: If you have power, you can use it for the common good.

JUDY, *overhearing this as she comes in, enters the fray.*

JUDY: Common good? What a joke. You wouldn't have the slightest inkling of what the common good was.

LIAM: Come and join the pile-on!

JUDY: The common good. What a joke. You'll do whatever your focus groups tell you will win an election.

LIAM: This from the lady who heads up a so called 'citizen's committee' that screams blue murder when we try and get some medium-density housing in her suburb so that people much less wealthy than she is can lead a better life. No, don't let them encroach on our leafy half-acres. Let them live fifty kilometres out on a Godforsaken blasted heath that bakes in summer, freezes in winter and has no community amenities and forces them to spend half their wages commuting an hour and a half every day on public transport. You really know something about the common good, don't you!

JUDY: We bought into that area because of what it offered. We're entitled to keep what we paid for.

LIAM: What you paid for? Fifteen years ago? Your house is worth three times what you paid for it now.

He jabs a finger in JUDY'*s direction.*

You've become rich because of it, but you still fight to the death to stop a handful of millennials sharing a little of what your urban paradise has to offer. Common good. Don't make me laugh. If I do get power I will crush you Pinot Gris socialists. I'll bring in a land tax that will cripple you and force you to sell. That's what I'll do with power. Actually use it in the common good.

JUDY: Everyone protects what they have!

LIAM: Even if they don't deserve it. But maybe you don't need to worry. Swinging playboy Charlie who serves the common good by making us buy shit we don't need, doesn't think I have what it takes to ever get that power. Don't you, Charlie. The only thing is that he hasn't told me why he thinks that, so I'm interested to hear.

CHARLIE: Because you're a nasty prick and always have been and that malignant nature of yours radiates out of you every time you appear on television.

LIAM: That's really brotherly.

CHARLIE: Okay, I'm your brother but that doesn't mean I have to like you and, believe me, I never have. I lost count of the near-drownings, the bashings, and the putdowns.

LIAM: Bloody little rabbit. Mummy's pet. For fuck's sake, we played the odd joke on you on you and gave you the odd bit of biff.

CHARLIE: The odd joke. Like the time you locked me out in the freezing cold in my pyjamas. If Daniel hadn't taken pity on me, against your orders, mind you, I would've frozen to death.

DANIEL: Charlie, it wasn't that bad.

CHARLIE: Well, it was for me and if you didn't have such a forgiving nature you'd remember a few things that happened to you. You beat him at table tennis and he throws a brick at your head. Fifteen stiches.

DANIEL: I did taunt him about it.

CHARLIE: That doesn't mean you deserve a brick hurled at you. Whenever he looked as if he might lose at Monopoly he just upended the board and ended the game.

LIAM: Once or twice.

CHARLIE: Every time! The only time we tried for an adult family holiday in Port Douglas a few years ago, you lost the toss for the best room and took it anyway. You refused to admit you were run out in beach cricket, didn't lift your finger once to share the workload, grabbed the last whole snapper on the menu when we went out—

JUDY: Didn't even bother to ask if anyone else might want it.

DANIEL: And insisted we watch your favourite shows on Netflix every night.

JUDY: Bloody André Rieu!

CHARLIE: You're a fucking horror, mate. Talk about Mum harbouring delusions. You're unelectable, mate! Face it.

LIAM: I don't let myself get fucked over like you guys and that makes me a monster? I'll be Premier.

CHARLIE: Check the latest polls, mate. You're a bad third!

LIAM: [*very angry*] Fuck off, the lot of you. I've got better things to do.

> *He whips out his iPhone as he storms out into the garden. It connects and we hear him talking loudly to one of his factional supporters.*

JUDY: [*to* CHARLIE] Good on you.

CHARLIE: He probably will get to be Premier.

JUDY: No.

DANIEL: He probably will. Forty percent of any population are latent fascists looking for a 'strong man' to solve their problems.

CHRISSY *comes inside looking worried.*

CHRISSY: What's wrong with Liam?

DANIEL: A few old grievances aired.

CHRISSY: I wish you wouldn't. When he's in a foul mood it always rebounds on me.

CHARLIE: Yeah. Sorry. Look, sorry, everyone. About Midge. Big mistake.

No-one disputes this.

I pissed off a good woman and got one who's … I still love her but she's totally unmanageable.

JUDY: Looking around at the marriages on show today, who can throw the first stone?

CHRISSY: What did you all say to Liam?

CHARLIE: That he needs to step up as a father and take some of the pressure off you.

CHRISSY: [*angry*] I'm quite capable of doing my own complaining! Just keep out of it. All of you. Okay, I'm not coping at the present. Everyone can see that, but I'm not a dishrag. I will fight my way out of it eventually and I will end up with four kids I'm proud of and a husband who might just achieve something worthwhile.

She stalks across and sits down on the other side of the room.

JUDY: Achieve something worthwhile?

DANIEL: He was right about us being NIMBYs. We have lucked on to a piece of valuable suburban paradise and we don't want to let anyone else share it.

JUDY: Daniel!

DANIEL: No fuck it, he was right! Would it really spoil our lives to have a few more people in well-designed affordable accommodation living nearby? Not really, and yet, like the pampered pricks we are we scream blue murder at the very thought.

CHARLIE: Jeez, bro. What's got into you?

DANIEL: Our brother is an awful bullying shit but maybe he has got a much stronger sense of fairness than any of us do. And maybe if he does get to be Premier the people who need a break might be more likely to get it!

JUDY: Suddenly the crusader?

DANIEL: [*suddenly flaring at* JUDY] If you want our marriage to be over, then fine!

    They all stare at him.

[*Still full rant*] Everything is all about you and your brilliant career and I'm just a little background hum!

JUDY: That's not true!

DANIEL: Well, that's how I feel. I'm going back full-time and becoming a qualified structural engineer. I'll still earn less that you will, but at least I'll be within striking distance!

JUDY: If that's what you want—

DANIEL: I know much more than most of the young fuckwits who are getting their degrees now. I'm sick of having to nurse them and fix their mistakes!

JUDY: That's fine. We can afford it.

DANIEL: I'm not taking a cent of your money!

JUDY: It's not an issue.

DANIEL: It is for me. I'll fund myself!

JUDY: How?

DANIEL: I'll do it. Okay?

JUDY: [*puzzled by his emphatic insistence*] Okay, whatever.

CHARLIE: Good for you, bro.

DANIEL: [*unloads on* CHARLIE] Don't call me bro! I'm Daniel!

CHARLIE: Okay.

    DANIEL *breathes deeply, outburst over.*

DANIEL: Okay, grievances aired so all we have to do now is ride out our mother's aria with a straight face. Have you warned Midge, Charlie?

CHARLIE: I have. But given Midge, I'm not entirely confident.

JUDY: Is it really helping her?

CHARLIE: What?

JUDY: Your mother. Letting this grotesque charade go on year after year?

CHARLIE: It's all she's got.

JUDY: Come on. She's got three sons she adores, three daughters-in-law she hates, what more could she want. I've had enough!

CHRISSY: [*from the other side of the room, with passion*] So have I! Year after year the sun shines out of her sons' arses and in goes the knife to us and we're supposed to grin and bear it. For what? To prop up her fragile ego. Fuck her! She's a monster.

CHARLIE: Ladies, let her have her one day.

CHRISSY: What aria do we have to endure this year?

DANIEL: Only the most difficult aria in opera history.

> *Beat.*

'Queen of the Night' from Mozart's *The Magic Flute*.

> *They all groan.*

CHARLIE: It's just once a year. Drink more champagne and grin and bear it.

> MIDGE *and* MONIQUE *come in from the garden chatting.* MONIQUE *turns brightly to the gathering.*

MONIQUE: Midge and I have been having a very nice chat in the garden about the best strategies to adopt to arrest ageing.

MIDGE: Some loose caboose steered Monique on to a face cream that turns wrinkles into canyons. I've lent her some of my Augustinus Bader.

MONIQUE: [*holding up a small bottle*] Your wife really knows what she's talking about, Charlie. One dab of Augustinus and I could almost hear my skin saying 'thank you'. I'm just going to pop inside and apply a little more before my little performance.

> MONIQUE *exits towards the bathroom. There's a tense silence. The others sense that there could be tension between* CHARLIE *and* MIDGE.

JUDY: I think I'll catch the last of the sunshine before the, er …

CHRISSY: Aria.

> JUDY, DANIEL *and* CHRISSY *leave for the garden.* MIDGE *holds baleful eye contact with* CHARLIE.

MIDGE: At least someone in this family appreciates me.

> *There's a silence.*

So. Do we have a window booking at Quay?

CHARLIE: No.

MIDGE: A good table at Ursula's?

CHARLIE: No.

MIDGE: Booked out?

CHARLIE: Don't know. I didn't call.

MIDGE: So where are we eating?

CHARLIE: A nice little pizza joint in Darlinghurst.

MIDGE: A pizza joint? You 're fucking joking.

CHARLIE: There's a Hungry Jack's next door if you prefer that.

MIDGE: I'm not amused, Charlie. I'm really not amused.

CHARLIE: If you want something better, perhaps you better call your friend Nick. I'm sure he could get you a front table at Aria.

MIDGE: You're not funny, Charlie.

CHARLIE: I wasn't trying to be funny.

MIDGE: If this is the kind of shit you're going to pull, our marriage isn't going to last long.

CHARLIE: That might be a very good thing.

MIDGE: You want our marriage to end?

CHARLIE: I'm too old for you, spend too much time with my mates, I hate the films and music you like, and you hate mine. And we can't talk about books because you don't read any. We even speak different languages.The only place it works between us is in the bedroom and I'll be sorry to lose that, but that will fade over time and then what are we left with?

MIDGE: Let's call it off? Just like that? With you showing no more emotion than a lobotomised frog?

CHARLIE: We made a mistake and you know it. Why not accept that and not go through prolonged agony?

MIDGE: I can't believe I'm hearing this.

[*Genuinely shocked*] I happen to love you.

CHARLIE: And I'm still besotted with you.

MIDGE: Then what's the problem?

CHARLIE: I've just mentioned about half a dozen but add to that the fact that no hotel room or resort is ever good enough for you, that no restaurant meal is up to expectations, that you're rude to waiters and shop assistants, that whatever happens to you is never your fault, that no matter how much attention you get it's never enough and that whatever's the latest fashion you have to have it.

MIDGE: I won't take second best. Ever.

CHARLIE: Why should you? The way you look has got you everything you wanted up to now and will for quite some time so why settle for anything less?

MIDGE: And in contrast to horrible little me, you're perfect.

CHARLIE: Far from it. I'm selfish, wilful, determined to do what I want to do—yeah all of that, but I don't demand the world fall at my feet, and I'm sick of watching little Miss Princess Pricetag expecting it to happen. I've reached my limit.

MIDGE: [*surprised*] Okay. If it's bugging you that much I can become more nush.

CHARLIE: Which in English means?

MIDGE: Sweetie-pie humble. I can change.

CHARLIE: You're not going to change, Midge. You're going to want the best of the best for as long as you can get it.

MIDGE: Look, if some bangable tart is flaunting a window seat and I haven't got one, I can't suddenly not hate it. She's not as hot as I am, so why the fuck is she there! It burns me from inside. But if it bugs you, I'll work at it. I'll change.

CHARLIE: Honey, you're not going to change. People never do. And same for me.

MIDGE: Okay, I'm a demanding bitch but I'm the demanding bitch that fell in love with you and I still am. You really want us to be over?

CHARLIE: If we do stay together, I warn you that if you try stuff on and I'll call you out. No more Mr Doormat.

MIDGE: You were never Mr Doormat.

CHARLIE: I had a sign on my forehead that said 'spineless'. But no more. No more no-limit Amex card so you can flash it at every piece of consumer trash that catches your fancy. You want to buy, you earn.

MIDGE: I can't ever earn what you do?

CHARLIE: You could! You're always talking about starting up your own chain of salons.

MIDGE: I need capital.

CHARLIE: I'll fund your first salon, then you're on your own.

MIDGE: You really think—

CHARLIE: You'll be great. Look, it's not just the money. I don't go to the office every day thinking about how much money I could earn.

A new account has come in. I've got to gather my team and come up with a concept that's brilliant and original enough to signal that I'm right up there near the top. That's the thrill. Life is not money, it's about challenge. You could start with next to nothing and build something you're proud of instead of wasting your time chatting with airheads over bilious-looking cocktails.

MIDGE *nods.*

MIDGE: Moaning about everything. Chattering about nothing. Airheads. I'm sick of them. You think I really could—

CHARLIE: You've got a lightning brain, honey. You can pick up a restaurant bill and spot the overcharge in a nanosecond.

MIDGE: Okay, okay. Well, that's exciting. New direction in life. Exciting. But you've got to give something too.

CHARLIE: What? No. Not kids. I've done kids.

MIDGE: Kids or I walk. That's my line in the sand.

CHARLIE: I'll think about it.

MIDGE: Not good enough.

CHARLIE: You'll be expanding your empire. How will you have time?

MIDGE: I'll find time. Yes or no?

CHARLIE: Okay. Okay.

MIDGE: Right. New directions. This is exciting. But pizza? That much of a new direction?

CHARLIE: It's the best pizza in Sydney. Four and a half stars in the *SMH*.

MIDGE: Really?

CHARLIE: The review said it was like eating a slice of heaven. The best! Okay! The best.

MIDGE: Okay, don't get aggressive.

[*Holding up her glass*] Here's to new directions.

They clink glasses and drink and suddenly and impulsively embrace. LIAM *storms in from the garden with his iPhone still up to his ear, sees* CHARLIE, *switches off his phone and heads straight for him.*

LIAM: That was bullshit! I was the one who let you back inside that night! Not Daniel.

CHARLIE: It was Daniel. And you tried to stop him. I probably would have lasted out the night but I would've been suffering from hypothermia.

LIAM: I would have let you back in.

CHARLIE: You know what? That was the worst moment in my life. Still is.

LIAM: Jesus. You were cold. Okay.

CHARLIE: It wasn't the cold. It was looking through the glass and seeing that you were loving watching me being scared shitless. That's what was so shocking. I suddenly realised there were some people who enjoyed watching others suffer. And that my brother was one of them. No empathy, no fellow feeling, just the joy of pure power over someone else's fate.

LIAM: Jesus, one mistake.

CHARLIE: Not a mistake. That was the essence of you. Power. Always will be. You're a prick.

LIAM: Think what you like, but in the last twenty minutes, two other caucus members have swung over to me because our fuckwitted Premier just put his foot in it yet again.

CHARLIE: You know what? I don't care if you become the Lord of All Creation as long as you stay away from me.

> LIAM *looks as if he's about to punch* CHARLIE *when* MONIQUE *sweeps in.*

MONIQUE: How do I look, Midge?

MIDGE: Great, absolutely great.

MONIQUE: The Augustinus is marvellous.

MIDGE: Five hundred bucks for fifty millilitres retail, but I get a few that fall off the back of a truck.

MONIQUE: Great to have someone streetwise in the family at last.

> MIDGE *moves across to her and makes some minor adjustments to her hair comb and takes out her beauty kit and does some quick work with blush and eyeliner. She shows* MONIQUE.

MONIQUE: Brilliant. What a great acquisition you're going to be.
[*To* LIAM *who is back on his phone*] Get off that damned phone and get everyone in here.

> LIAM *moves towards the door but before he reaches it,* DANIEL, CHRISSY *and* JUDY *come in from the garden.*

MONIQUE: Daniel. Have you got the sheet music?

DANIEL: Yes.

MONIQUE: Then let's get started. Please take a seat, everyone. Take a seat. I've got a few words to say and then … the aria!

Her eyes shine brightly as she watches everyone find a seat.

Today I'm going to sing the aria that I used as the audition piece that got me into the Conservatorium. So now for your enjoyment, Mozart's 'The Queen of the Night' from *The Magic Flute*.

DANIEL *starts playing and the aria begins.* MONIQUE *has a reasonable voice that has obviously been trained but it's soon apparent that she's not up to the difficulty level of the aria. When it's over there's embarrassed silence, then strained applause led by her three boys.*

Thank you. Thank you. I was struggling a little in the higher register but I got there. Thank you. Now, before we go our separate ways, sometimes it falls to the matriarch of the family to break some sad news. And I take no joy in saying it. Today, sadly, Daniel confided in me that his marriage has run its course.

JUDY *frowns in a state of semi-shock and stares at* DANIEL, *still at the piano, who looks mortified.*

Sometimes in our preoccupation with our own success, we can miss the pain our partner is going through until, as in this case, it's too late. But enough of that. As Kevin would say, 'It is what it is.'

JUDY: [*to* DANIEL] Our marriage run its course?

DANIEL: You were the one who seemed to want it to be over.

JUDY: I didn't mean it!

MONIQUE: Sadly, Daniel does.

JUDY: What's she talking about?

DANIEL: [*to* JUDY] Do you still want me as a husband or not!

JUDY: Of course I do! What in the hell is she talking about?

MONIQUE: Stand up for yourself, Daniel. Tell her it's over!

JUDY: What's going on?

DANIEL: [*wrestles with the truth*] The truth is that Mum offered me money to pay for me to qualify as a structural engineer and for a moment I was tempted—

JUDY: What!?

DANIEL: If I split up with you.

JUDY: You were tempted.

DANIEL: For a moment!

JUDY: [*turning on* MONIQUE] You bloody old witch!

[*To* DANIEL] You were going to leave!

DANIEL: [*to* JUDY] I was considering it.

JUDY: Why?

DANIEL: [*erupting*] Because you're bossy and irritating and annoying and self-centred and take it for granted that I'll always be there to take orders and sometimes I do get sick of it! Okay?

JUDY: [*erupting in turn*] And you are without faults? Sullen, resentful, passive aggressive. 'Yes I'll see to it, dear'—and you never do and I have to finally deal with it. Every time! You were walking out on me?

DANIEL: Just for a minute!

JUDY: Well, fuck you. And no more of this bullshit from your bloody mother that I somehow stopped your glorious concert career! Okay, you could play but hey, you were never going to be another Daniel Barenboim and you knew it. Okay, you graduated from the Con, which is more than your mother ever did—

MONIQUE: I did!

JUDY: Let's cut the bullshit, Monique. Your 'Queen of the Night' was embarrassing. We squirmed.

CHARLIE: Judy!

JUDY: I've had enough! She didn't even get into the Con, let alone graduate. She failed her audition three times.

DANIEL: Judy!

JUDY: Tell the truth, Monique. You're a fucking fraud.

JUDY *indicates the fashion photos around the wall.*

You failed your audition three times.

MONIQUE *stands there in state of shock.*

CHARLIE: Judy, don't do this!

JUDY: I've done it!

[*To* DANIEL] And if you want out of our marriage then take your mother's pieces of silver and don't ever come near me again!

DANIEL: I'm doing the course part-time! I'm not taking a cent of her money!

JUDY: If you do decide to come home, take a taxi because I'm taking the car. I can't stand to be in this bloody house a second longer. Oh, and our daughter is going to Concord High whether you like it or not. Look what her present school turned your mother into and ask yourself whether any sane parent would send their kid there.

DANIEL: [*following her as she moves towards the front door*] No, no. I'm fine with that. Concord High is the right choice.

The front door slams. There is silence as DANIEL *returns to the room looking distressed. We hear a car start up outside and screech down the drive.* CHRISSY *gets up and confronts a still shell-shocked* MONIQUE.

CHRISSY: And while we're at it, Monique. I know you think all I should be doing it is supporting your bloody son on his path to power? Well, guess what. That's all over. If he doesn't shape up and start remembering he has four kids, I'm out of there and he can see what it's like to look after them. And see how he copes then. You get a taxi too, Liam.

LIAM: Okay, okay, I'll spend more time with the kids.

CHRISSY: You'll have to because I'm going to go back to work whether you like it or not! And, Monique, Judy was right. Your 'Queen of the Night' was bloody awful!

She leaves. MONIQUE *is still standing there in a state of shock. She turns to her three sons.*

MONIQUE: All right, I'm not a Rita Streich, but for my age, it was good.

She looks around for confirmation. There's an awkward silence.

Perhaps it was a degree of difficulty more than I should have tried but for my age … Midge?

MIDGE: Your make-up was perfect. Perfect. Just the right light too.

MONIQUE: The performance, Midge. The performance.

MIDGE: Actually, love, it was pretty shit, but you tried. That's guts. You tried.

MONIQUE *looks up at her portrait as a younger woman.*

MONIQUE: That last audition. I was so close. They told me. So close.

There's a silence.

All right. 'Queen of the Night' was stretching me but last year my 'One Fine Day'. *Madame Butterfly*. That was good.

Again there's silence.

It was good.

DANIEL: It was better, Mum.

MONIQUE: Better. Still bad, just better.

There's silence. Suddenly she has a burst of rage.

I don't care what any of you think! That last audition I was on the verge of making it!

CHARLIE: Mum, you were a good singer but not great. We all usually think we're better than we are.

MONIQUE: They asked me to try and again next year and I would have made it! But then came Kevin. And I had to choose and I made the right choice.

She sits down and tears start to fall. CHARLIE *sits down beside her.*

CHARLIE: You did, Mum, and we all love that you did make that choice …

MONIQUE: Okay, 'Queen of the Night' was ambitious. But it wasn't terrible.

CHARLIE: No, it wasn't. But it wasn't as good as you thought it was. We all do it. I'm not the great creative mind I try and tell myself I am. I can spot young talent and I hire it. And that's fine. Liam is never going—okay, we won't go there. Daniel still half-believes he had the talent to be the next Daniel Barenboim. The human ego is very fragile. We couldn't get by without some delusions.

MONIQUE: Delusions. So you all really think I'm a ridiculous old lady with ridiculous delusions.

DANIEL: Your voice is good, Mum. Just not great.

MONIQUE *gets up and walks towards the garden.*

MONIQUE: Damned with faint praise.

She leaves. Her sons look at each other.

CHARLIE: Oh Jesus.

DANIEL: Yeah.

LIAM: [*to* DANIEL] Did Judy *have* to destroy her like that?

DANIEL: And your Chrissy didn't add fuel to the flames?

LIAM: Bloody oversensitive, both of them. All mothers are a bit biased about their sons.

> MIDGE *laughs.*

MIDGE: A bit biased? You guys could shit on the carpet and your mother would call you charmingly unpredictable.

CHARLIE: She's not that bad.

MIDGE: Sorry. You've been spoiled rotten and your poor wives have had to pay.

LIAM: All right. I have been a bit obsessive. I've got the message.

> *At that moment, an angry* MONIQUE *storms back into the room and stares at her sons.*

DANIEL: Mum, we are sorry it ended like this.

MONIQUE: [*to* DANIEL *and* LIAM] It needn't have—if any, you two had had the guts to stand up to those wives of yours. Daniel! I couldn't believe my ears. You're skulking back to that bully of a wife of yours, tail between your legs!

DANIEL: Mum, I—

MONIQUE: You never did have any backbone. And Liam? You're going to suddenly become a house husband. Give up the thing you've fought so hard for and become a pussy-whipped domestic servant?

LIAM: I'm still going after the top job. I'm just going to help with those kids a little bit more —

MONIQUE: Because she's incapable of controlling her own kids! Charlie's the only one of you who wouldn't put up with a second-rate wife and has found himself a good one at last.

CHARLIE: Mum, we know you're upset about what happened today—

MONIQUE: You're damned right I'm upset. My aria was still damned good for a woman of my age and you boys stood there and let those wives of yours ridicule me. Okay, I wasn't at my top but I can do it! Get back to the piano, Daniel. I'm going to get it right this time!

DANIEL: Mum!

MONIQUE: Just give me the intro.

LIAM: Mum, no!

MONIQUE: The intro. I'm going to show you all that I can do it before you skulk back to your wives. Daniel, the intro, please.

DANIEL: Mum. No. No.

MONIQUE: I would have made it. They begged me to come back and audition again next year.

DANIEL: Yes, I'm sure you would've.

MONIQUE: I can hear the doubt in your voice, Daniel. Back to the piano and play that intro.

DANIEL: Mum. I'm going home. My marriage isn't perfect but I still love her and we'll work it through.

MONIQUE: She's finished with you! Didn't you hear her?

DANIEL: She was mad. And she had reason. It'll be fine.

LIAM: I'm off too.

MONIQUE: [*to* LIAM] I'll give you some aprons from the kitchen. You're going to need them!

> LIAM *kisses his reluctant mother on the cheek.*

LIAM: Thanks for a lovely afternoon.

> LIAM *high-fives* DANIEL. *Hesitates and high-fives* CHARLIE.

I would have let you back in! I'm not a psychopath.

CHARLIE: I got you wrong, bro. You're just a cuddly little Shih Tzu.

LIAM: Get stuffed.

> *He leaves, getting his iPhone back to his ear after he dials.*

Gary? Let's talk in about half an hour. Great news today. Our bloody Premier stuffed up again!

MONIQUE: Daniel, please. Let me try it once more.

> DANIEL *kisses his mother on the cheek, waves at* CHARLIE *and* MIDGE *and leaves.*

I wasn't really that bad was I, Midge? Midge?

MIDGE: Your make-up was world-class.

CHARLIE: Bye, Mum.

> *He kisses her on the cheek.*

We all love you. Well, most of us. Okay, maybe you did indulge us but that's a hell of a lot better than being ignored and abused.

MONIQUE: You boys are all I have left. Don't ever desert me. I'd have
    nothing. Nothing.
CHARLIE: We won't.

> *She watches as they leave. She sighs, and slumps into a chair
> with an air of defeated melancholy, but after a few seconds
> gets a look of resolve in her face. She gets up and takes out
> her iPhone and scans through her Spotify playlists. She clicks a
> selection and sits back down and listens as Diana Damrau sings
> 'The Queen of the Night'. She gets up from her chair and starts
> to sing along with her, admits defeat, and sits down again and
> listens. Then shrugs.*

MONIQUE: [*standing and shouting above the music to Diana*] Not
    everyone can be one in a million! And if I had've done that fourth
    audition. Who knows! Who bloody knows!

> *She sits back down and listens as Diana sings on.*

At any rate, I've still got my boys!

THE END

DAVID WILLIAMSON'S

ARIA

ENSEMBLE THEATRE
DIRECTED BY JANINE WATSON
24 JANUARY 2025 – 15 MARCH 2025
WORLD PREMIERE

Ensemble Theatre proudly acknowledges the Cammeraigal people of the Eora nation as customary owners of the land on which we work and share our stories. We pay our respects to Elders past and present.

CAST

TAMARA LEE BAILEY MIDGE
ROWAN DAVIE CHARLIE
DANIELLE KING JUDY
TRACY MANN MONIQUE
SUZANNAH MCDONALD CHRISSY
SAM O'SULLIVAN DANIEL
JACK STARKEY-GILL LIAM

CREATIVES

PLAYWRIGHT DAVID WILLIAMSON AO
DIRECTOR JANINE WATSON
ASSISTANT DIRECTOR ANNA HOUSTON
SET & COSTUME DESIGNER ROSE MONTGOMERY
LIGHTING DESIGNER MATT COX
COMPOSER & SOUND DESIGNER DAVID BERGMAN
OPERATIC VOICE COACH DONNA BALSON
STAGE MANAGER LAUREN TULLOH
ASSISTANT STAGE MANAGER BELLA WELLSTEAD
COSTUME SUPERVISOR RENATA BESLIK

RUNNING TIME 1 HOUR 40 MINUTES NO INTERVAL
REC. AGES 12+
ADULT THEMES, COARSE LANGUAGE

ABOUT ENSEMBLE THEATRE

Ensemble Theatre is the longest continuously running professional theatre company in Australia and is committed to collaborating with exceptional playwrights and creative talent to present the best international plays, modern classics and new Australian works.

PLAYWRIGHT'S NOTE

Most of us need some mild delusions about ourselves to help us get through life. That we're a tad more personable, intelligent and talented than perhaps we really are. Monique, the pivotal character in ARIA, being more than a touch narcissistic, needs delusions to prop up her huge but fragile ego. She believes she was destined to become an international opera star until the duties of motherhood intervened, but to compensate for this loss she is convinced her three sons are nigh on perfect. She believes however that these brilliant sons deserved much better wives, and leaves her daughters-in-law in no doubt about her feelings, but as the events of the play unfold, it becomes clear that the daughters-in-law have finally had enough.

I've been fascinated with narcissistic personality disorders even since my days at Melbourne University studying psychology. Basically narcissists are hugely self-centred and believe the rest of humanity is only there to heap praise on them. Other people's lives are of no interest to them. But in ARIA I wanted to tackle the moment when a narcissistic personality's delusions are put under severe threat.

I loved writing all the characters in the play but especially Monique, she's magnificently insufferable, and I can't help loving the way she indomitably refuses to be shattered, but reshapes her delusions and soldiers on at the end of the play.

You can inflict flesh wounds on a narcissist but like a shape shifter they rise again to haunt us. Who would have thought a man who encouraged insurrection because he couldn't accept that he lost an election, would bounce back to become the most powerful man in the world?

Monique's daughters-in-law might have won the battle but they might not have won the war.

DAVID WILLIAMSON AO
PLAYWRIGHT

DIRECTOR'S NOTE

I first encountered ARIA by David Williamson when I was asked to present a scene from it for a fundraising event at Ensemble Theatre. After working on just four pages of the play I told Mark Kilmurry that if they were programming ARIA I wanted to direct it. It isn't surprising, given the immense wit and intelligence so typical of David's work, how it leaps off the page. The characters and relationships are so vivid, so recognisable and intriguingly flawed. And very funny.

The structure of the play struck me as incredibly exciting - one afternoon, a family gathering, a special event. All taking place in the piano room of Monique's opulent home, it plays out in real time without scene changes. The atmosphere is charged with ego and discord as long suppressed grievances find their way to the surface. I was drawn in by the extreme dynamics of these characters when they are forced to engage with one another. I wanted to direct these scenes, to tell this story. The savage social satire is grounded in an incisive vision of contemporary Australian class and social politics. David uses the protagonist Monique as a beacon of unremitting power, whose assertive dominance is a cover for deep fault lines in her relationships.

I think ARIA is one of the pinnacles in David's incomparable and prolific career. It has all the humour and laughter so beloved of his plays while fearlessly staring privilege and hypocrisy directly in the eye. In ARIA he centres four complex intelligent female roles at the heart of the story and has a wonderful time positioning them opposite deeply flawed male characters who have enjoyed immense economic advantage.

It is always an honour for me to be entrusted by a writer with a new work. And when that writer is a giant in the world of playwriting it is a major career highlight. However, the real privilege is in the artistic collaboration that we've formed as the play is readied for production. How encouraging, kind, and supportive David has been. He's always available and open to questions and discussions. His passion for his work is evident in his energy, his research, his clarity of vision.

Our creative team and cast are magnificent. I'm so excited to bring ARIA to the stage for its World Premiere. My heartiest thanks to David and Mark for giving me this opportunity.

JANINE WATSON
DIRECTOR

DAVID WILLIAMSON AO
PLAYWRIGHT

Ensemble Theatre: Premieres include: THE GREAT DIVIDE, RHINESTONE REX AND MISS MONICA, CRUNCH TIME, THE BIG TIME, SORTING OUT RACHEL, ODD MAN OUT, JACK OF HEARTS, DREAM HOME, CRUISE CONTROL, HAPPINESS, WHEN DAD MARRIED FURY, NOTHING PERSONAL, AT ANY COST? (Co-written with Mohamed Khadra), LET THE SUNSHINE, LOTTE'S GIFT, OPERATOR, FLATFOOT (with Christine Dunstan Productions), A CONVERSATION, FACE TO FACE. Griffin Theatre Company: FAMILY VALUES. La Boite Theatre/Noosa Long Weekend: STRINGS UNDER MY FINGERS. La Mama Theatre: CREDENTIALS, THE REMOVALISTS, THE COMING OF STORK. Melbourne Theatre Company: RUPERT, DON PARTIES ON, SCARLET O'HARA AT THE CRIMSON PARROT, BIRTHRIGHTS, SONS OF CAIN, THE CLUB, JUGGLERS THREE. Nimrod: CELLULOID HEROES, TRAVELLING NORTH. Old Tote: WHAT IF YOU DIED TOMORROW? Playbox: SANCTUARY. Pram Factory: DON'S PARTY. State Theatre Company South Australia: THE PUZZLE, A HANDFUL OF FRIENDS, THE DEPARTMENT. Sydney Theatre Company: INFLUENCE, AMIGOS, SOULMATES, UP FOR GRABS (with Melbourne Theatre Company), THE GREAT MAN, CORPORATE VIBES (with Queensland Theatre), THIRD WORLD BLUES, HERETIC, DEAD WHITE MALES, SIREN, EMERALD CITY, THE PERFECTIONIST. Queensland Theatre: NEARER THE GODS, MANAGING CARMEN, AFTER THE BALL, BRILLIANT LIES, MONEY & FRIENDS. Film and Television include: FACE TO FACE, BALIBO, ON THE BEACH, BRILLIANT LIES, SANCTUARY, EMERALD CITY, TRAVELLING NORTH, THE PERFECTIONIST, THE LAST BASTION, PHAR LAP, THE YEAR OF LIVING DANGEROUSLY, GALLIPOLI, THE CLUB, DON'S PARTY, ELIZA FRASER, THE REMOVALISTS, STORK. Awards: Some of David's many awards include twelve Australian Writers' Guild Awards, five Australian Film Institute Awards for Best Screenplay and, in 1996, the

United Nations Association of Australia Media Peace Award. David has received four honorary doctorates and been made an Officer of the Order of Australia, as well as having been named one of Australia's Living National Treasures.

JANINE WATSON
DIRECTOR

Directing Credits: Ensemble Theatre: COLDER THAN HERE, ALONE IT STANDS, A BROADCAST COUP, NEARER THE GODS, STILL UNQUALIFIED, UNQUALIFIED. Bell Shakespeare: THE COMEDY OF ERRORS, ROMEO AND JULIET. Redline Productions: FIERCE, CRIMES OF THE HEART, DOLORES (co-director). Acting Credits: Ensemble Theatre: A VIEW FROM THE BRIDGE. Bell Shakespeare: KING LEAR, THE DREAM. Griffin Theatre: THE HAPPY PRINCE. Little Ones Theatre: DANGEROUS LIAISONS, DRACULA. Sport For Jove: THREE SISTERS. Film: THE CODE. Television: THE SECRETS SHE KEEPS, NEIGHBOURS, THAT'S NOT ME. Training: National Theatre Drama School (Melbourne). Awards: Sandra Bates Directing Award 2016. Sydney Theatre Award – Best Lead Female Performance THE HAPPY PRINCE 2019. GLUG Award – Best Supporting Actress A VIEW FROM THE BRIDGE 2017.

ANNA HOUSTON
ASSISTANT DIRECTOR

Director credits: Griffin Theatre (Lysicrates Prize): NO NEED TO HIDE A LIGHT WHEN IT SHINES LIKE HERS. Old Fitz Theatre: CYPRUS AVENUE, THE LONESOME WEST. Seymour Centre: ARLINGTON. Acting Credits: Bell Shakespeare: THE SERVANT OF TWO MASTERS, AS YOU LIKE IT, THE TAMING OF THE SHREW. Belvoir Street

Theatre: HEDDA GABLER. B Sharp: THE
MERCHANT OF VENICE, BEYOND THE NECK.
Darlinghurst Theatre Company: ALL MY SONS,
VENUS IN FUR. Griffin Theatre: JUMP FOR
JORDAN. Perth Theatre Company: TENDER
NAPALM, BLACKBIRD. Sport For Jove: OF MICE
AND MEN. National Theatre of UK: WAR HORSE.
Film: EVENT ZERO. Television: AMAZING GRACE,
A PLACE TO CALL HOME, ALL SAINTS, BLUE
HEELERS. Training: Ecole Philippe Gaulier (Paris).
National Institute of Dramatic Art: BA Acting.

TAMARA LEE BAILEY
MIDGE

ARIA is Tamara's Ensemble Theatre debut. Bell
Shakespeare: KING LEAR. Michael Cassel: HARRY
POTTER AND THE CURSED CHILD. Sport For
Jove: RICHARD III, HENRY IV, THIRD AGE
PROJECT, SECOND AGE PROJECT. Montague
Basement: THE GREAT AUSTRALIAN PLAY.
Victorian College of the Arts: OTHELLO, F***ING
A, FEFU AND HER FRIENDS, THE CHERRY
ORCHARD, THEBAN DOLLS. Australian Theatre
for Young People: INTERSECTION. Television:
NCIS: SYDNEY. ABC Children: MIKKI VS THE
WORLD (Season 2). Training: Victorian College of
the Arts: Bachelor of Fine Arts (Acting).

ROWAN DAVIE
CHARLIE

Ensemble Theatre: NEARER THE GODS, AWAY
(READING). Bell Shakespeare: ROMEO AND JULIET,
with The Players: MACBETH, SUCH SWEET
SORROW, DOUBLE TROUBLE, HAMLET: OUT OF
JOINT. La Boite: OR FOREVER HOLD YOUR PEACE.
Redline Productions: THE WIND IN THE

UNDERGROUND, CRIMES OF HEART. Monkey Baa Theatre: ANGELS IN AMERICA: MILLENNIUM APPROACHES. Old Fitz Theatre: INFINITY TASTER. New Theatre: AFTER THE DANCE. Film: THAT'S NOT ME. Television: HOME AND AWAY, APPLES NEVER FALL, TEN POUND POMS, CLOUDY RIVER, A PLACE TO CALL HOME. Awards: 2014 NOMINATION Tenerife International Film Festival - Best Supporting Actor, LIFE THROUGH A LENS. Training: QUT, LARRY MOSS, SITI COMPANY.

DANIELLE KING
JUDY

ARIA is Danielle's Ensemble Theatre debut. ATYP: ISHMEAL AND THE RETURN OF THE DUGONGS. Almedia Theatre: RICHARD II, CORIOLANUS. Bell Shakespeare: HENRY V. CDP: THE 91 STOREY TREE- HOUSE. Darlinghurst: MACBETH. Chichester: ON THE RAZZLE. Compass Theatre Co: THE RIVALS. Don't Look Now & KXT: NIGHT SLOWS DOWN. Exeter: TWO GENTLEMEN OF VERONA. Flight Path Theatre: IN TRANSIT. ICA: JEFF KOONS. Merrigong Theatre Co: A MIDSUMMER'S NIGHT DREAM. Many Moons: SAID AND DONE. Outhouse Theatre Co: 4 MINUTES 12 SECONDS. Red Lion: SIMPATICO. Salisbury Playhouse: THE TAMING OF THE SHREW. Shalom Theatre Co: THE MAN IN THE ATTIC. Sphinx: AS YOU LIKE IT. Sport for Jove: NO END OF BLAME, AWAY, THE TAMING OF THE SHREW, HAMLET, THE TEMPEST, TWELFTH NIGHT, MACBETH, THE LIBERTINE. The Studio: THE ART OF SUCCESS, THE LOWER DEPTHS. Sydney Theatre Company: THE TEMPEST, NOISES OFF. The White Bear: TRANCE. White Box Theatre: TABLE, BLACKROCK. York Theatre Royal: TWELFTH NIGHT, HAY FEVER. Young Vic: SLEEPING BEAUTY. Film: ECHO PINES, HEARTS AND BONES, FELONY, THE GATHERING STORM. Television: THE TWELVE, WELLMANIA,

DOCTOR DOCTOR, THE LET DOWN, HOME & AWAY, BAD GIRLS, HOLBY CITY. Awards: Best Actress in an Independent Production Sydney Theatre Critics Award 2011: THE LIBERTINE.

TRACY MANN
MONIQUE

Ensemble Theatre: RELATIVELY SPEAKING, AT ANY COST, HEIDI CHRONICLES. Belvoir Street Theatre: THE CURIOUS INCIDENT OF THE DOG IN THE NIGHT-TIME, MY BRILLIANT CAREER. Force Majeure: NEVER DID ME ANY HARM. Really Useful: THE GRADUATE. Seymour Centre: MADE TO MEASURE. State Theatre SA: THE REMOVALISTS. Sydney Theatre Co: BLITHE SPIRIT, HOME I'M DARLING, NOISES OFF, EMBERS. Film: ANGEL OF MINE, TOP END WEDDING, FELONY, ANY QUESTIONS FOR BEN, HATING ALISON ASHLEY, THE CUP. Television: THE TWELVE Season 3, TOP END BUB, FIVE BEDROOMS, LATECOMERS, ROSEHAVEN, WONDERLAND, LAID, RAKE, EAST OF EVERYTHING, THE BRUSH OFF, SWORD OF HONOUR, CYCLONE TRACY, SWEET & SOUR, THE BOX. Awards: AFI Best Actress for HARD KNOCKS, LOGIE 1986 Most Popular Actress for SWORD OF HONOUR.

SUZANNAH MCDONALD
CHRISSY

ARIA is Suzannah's Ensemble Theatre debut. Bell Shakespeare Company: THE COMEDY OF ERRORS. FortyFivedownstairs: FAR AWAY. Griffin Theatre: SMASHED. Kage Physical Theatre: THE DAY THE WORLD TURNED UPSIDE DOWN. Kei Takei's Moving Earth Orient Sphere (Japan): RICE FIELDS. Malthouse Theatre: THE ODYSSEY. Monkey Baa Theatre: A VOYAGE TO THE DEEP.

Film: TURKEY SHOOT, THE LAST RACE, ONE
NIGHT. Television: HOUSE OF GODS, READY FOR
THIS, CROWNIES, THE POLITICALLY INCORRECT
PARENTING SHOW, CITY HOMICIDE, THE JESTER,
UNDERBELLY: TALE OF TWO CITIES, A MODEL
DAUGHTER: THE KILLING OF CAROLINE BYRNES,
DANCE ACADEMY, ALL SAINTS. Training: Victorian
College of the Arts Bachelor of Dramatic Arts
2001.

SAM O'SULLIVAN
DANIEL

Ensemble Theatre: MIDNIGHT MURDER AT
HAMLINGTON HALL, NEARER THE GODS, THE
NORMAN CONQUESTS, A HISTORY OF FALLING
THINGS, MY ZINC BED. Belvoir St. Theatre: KILL
THE MESSENGER. Cathode Ray Tube: A STEADY
RAIN. Critical Stages: CAPTURE THE FLAG. Cross
Pollinate: JOURNEY'S END. Darlinghurst Theatre:
CONSTELLATIONS. Griffin Theatre: MUSIC. King's
Cross Theatre: WINK. Outhouse Theatre:
CONSENT. Pantsguys: PUNK ROCK. Mirror Mirror:
HILT. Mophead Productions: PLATONOV. Seymour
Centre: MADE TO MEASURE. Sport For Jove: NO
END OF BLAME. Rock Surfers: THE REMOVALISTS,
SPROUT. Film: CROSSING PATHS. Television:
CLASS OF '07, AMAZING GRACE, ON THE ROPES,
BLACK COMEDY, HOME & AWAY, WONDERLAND,
PACKED TO THE RAFTERS, FAST TRACKS. Short
Film: WHEN HAROLD MET ARNOLD, REFUSED
CLASSIFICATION, LITTLE LOVE, THE BELFAST
BOYS, CONCESSION. Awards: ATYP Foundation
Commission: CHARLIE PILGRIM. Sydney Theatre
Award Nominations: PUNK ROCK, JOURNEY'S
END, THE BLOCK UNIVERSE, CHARLIE PILGRIM.
Training: The National Institute of Dramatic Art.
As a writer, Sam's works include: Ensemble
Theatre: MCGUFFIN PARK, BOXING DAY BBQ.
Australian Theatre for Young People: CHARLIE

PILGRIM. Cross Pollinate: THE BLOCK UNIVERSE. Redline Productions: THE WIND IN THE UNDERGROUND. Rogue Projects: YOU'RE NOT SPECIAL.

JACK STARKEY-GILL
LIAM

ARIA is Jack's Ensemble Theatre debut. Theatre: Bell Shakespeare: MACBETH, THE PLAYERS. CDP: THE 52 STOREY TREEHOUSE. Emma Sandall: AN AMBIVALENT WOMAN OF 37. Don't Look Away Theatre: A PROPERTY OF THE CLAN. The Old Fitz Theatre: INFINITY CHASER. Film: MARLEY, SOMEONE. Television: NEIGHBOURS. Voice Director: Bell Shakespeare: KING LEAR, A MIDSUMMER NIGHT'S DREAM, TWELFTH NIGHT, ROMEO AND JULIET, THE PLAYERS. Voice, Dialect & Text Coach: Michael Cassel Group: MARY POPPINS. Sydney Theatre Company: CONSTELLATIONS. Emma Sandall: AN AMBIVALENT WOMAN OF 37. National Institute of Dramatic Art: SANDAIME RICHARD, KINDNESS, FESTEN, MACBETH. ACA: THE LIBERTINE. Director: SAS: DOGG'S HAMLET, THE CAGEBIRDS. Training: Victorian College of the Arts. The National Institute of Dramatic Art.

ROSE MONTGOMERY
SET AND COSTUME DESIGNER

Canberra Theatre: CHIAROSCURO, ME RIGHT NOW. National Institute of Dramatic Art Theatres: THE WAY OF THE WORLD, THE COLBY SISTERS OF PITTSBURGH, PENNSYLVANIA. Redfern Pop Up Theatre: THIS MODERN COIL. Charing Cross Theatre: MARIE CURIE THE MUSICAL. Fortune Theatre: OPERATION MINCEMEAT THE MUSICAL (Graphics Designer). The Old Vic: SYLVIA (Graphics

Designer). Immersive International: THE GREAT GATSBY NYC (Graphics Designer). Punchdrunk: THE BURNT CITY (Head of Graphics). Theatrical Niche Touring Company UK: UNCLE VANYA. Film: GLOVE, SVENGALI, THOR: LOVE AND THUNDER (Set Decoration Assistant), ALL ABOUT E. Television: THE GREAT SEASON 3 (Production Design Assistant), PIECES OF HER (Set Decoration Assistant), THE HOME TEAM (Props Master), HOME AND AWAY (Art Department and Wardrobe). Awards: Loudon Sainthill Memorial Scholarship 2021, ABC RN TOP 5 ARTS 2020, JMK Theatre Award Finalist 2020, BAFTA Connects 2020, Sydney Opera House Made Scholarship 2018. Training Institutions: National Institute of Dramatic Art and University of Technology Sydney.

MATT COX
LIGHTING DESIGNER

Ensemble Theatre: UNCLE VANYA, A CHRISTMAS CAROL, BOXING DAY BBQ, A VIEW FROM THE BRIDGE, A BROADCAST COUP, THE CARETAKER, NEARER THE GODS, DIPLOMACY, MURDER ON THE WIRELESS, ALONE IT STANDS, BENEFACTORS, SUMMER OF HAROLD. Bangarra Dance Theatre: WARU JOURNEY OF THE SMALL TURTLE, DUBBOO, ONE'S COUNTRY, OUR LAND PEOPLE STORIES, BLAK, BELONG. Duet Group: DIVAS. Hayes Theatre Company: SHE LOVES ME. Louise Withers and Associates: THE MOUSETRAP, A MURDER IS ANNOUNCED. Soft Tread: WHARF REVUE 2023: PRIDE IN PREJUDICE, WHARF REVUE 2022: LOOKING FOR ALBANESE, WHARF REVUE 2021: CAN OF WORMS. Sydney Chamber Opera: HIS MUSIC BURNS. Sydney Theatre Company: WHARF REVUE 2020; WHARF REVUE 2019; WHARF REVUE 2018; RUBY MOON. Tinderbox Productions: DAVID SUCHET, POIROT and more.

DAVID BERGMAN
COMPOSER AND SOUND DESIGNER

Ensemble Theatre: MEMORY OF WATER. Bangarra Dance Company: KULKA, SANDSONG, SPIRIT, KNOWLEDGE GROUND. Bell Shakespeare: TWELFTH NIGHT, THE LOVERS. Belvoir Street Theatre: BLUE, SCENES FROM THE CLIMATE ERA, INTO THE WOODS, AT WHAT COST? Griffin Theatre Company: GREEN PARK, SUPERHEROES. Michael Cassel Group: DEAR EVAN HANSEN. Sydney Theatre Company: THE PICTURE OF DORIAN GRAY, STRANGE CASE OF DR JEKYLL AND MR HYDE, JULIUS CAESAR, MURIEL'S WEDDING: THE MUSICAL, THE HANGING. The Australian Ballet: OSCAR. Victorian Opera: IDOMENEO. West Australian Opera: RUSALKA. Awards: David has won two Sydney Theatre Awards including for best Stage Design of a Mainstage Production for THE PICTURE OF DORIAN GRAY, and for Best Sound Design of a Mainstage Production for GREEN PARK. Training: National Institute of Dramatic Art.

DONNA BALSON
OPERATIC VOICE COACH

Ensemble Theatre: MASTER CLASS. Opera Australia: Guest Coach; performer in PETER GRIMES, FIDDLER ON THE ROOF, THE LITTLE MERMAID, MADAMA BUTTERFLY, NABUCCO, etc. Opera Queensland: Guest Coach; performer in CENERENTOLA, COSI FAN TUTTE, WALTZING OUR MATILDA. Opera Canterbury: TOSCA, FORZA DEL DESTINO. Opera Greenville, SC: MEFISTOFELE. Opera Frankfurt: COME AND GO, JENUFA. Opera Lanka: LA TRAVIATA. Frankfurter Kammeroper: IL CAMBIALE DI MATRIMONIO. Operaworks NY: THE SEAGULL, SALOME; Long

Beach Opera at the Getty Museum: FRESHWATER. Concerts with: American Chamber Ensemble, China National Orchestra, Ensemble Moderne, Fires of New York, Hessischer Rundfunk Orchestra, Jacksonville Symphony, National Chorale at Lincoln Centre, Netherlands Radio Symphony, New England Symphonic Ensemble at Carnegie Hall, Residentie Orchestra Den Haag, Symphony of the Americas. Vocal Consultancy: Frankfurt Ballet (William Forsythe) ISABEL'S DANCE, BBC films ETERNITY MAN. Teaching: Hofstra University, New York; Sydney Conservatorium.

LAUREN TULLOH
STAGE MANAGER

Lauren is Ensemble Theatre's Resident Stage Manager. Ensemble Theatre: MCGUFFIN PARK, UNCLE VANYA, SWITZERLAND, ALONE IT STANDS, THE MEMORY OF WATER, MR BAILEY'S MINDER, CLYDE'S, A BROADCAST COUP, THE CARETAKER, THE ONE, A LETTER FOR MOLLY, KILLING KATIE: CONFESSIONS OF A BOOKCLUB, THE WOMAN IN BLACK, THE APPLETON LADIES' POTATO RACE (2021 regional tour), OUTDATED, THE LAST WIFE, THE LAST FIVE YEARS, MARJORIE PRIME, THE PLANT, BETRAYAL. Hayes Theatre Company: REWIRED: MUSICALS REIMAGINED, AMERICAN PSYCHO, HIGH FIDELITY, ASSASSINS, CALAMITY JANE, THE FANTASTICKS, VIOLET. National Theatre of Parramatta: QUEEN FATIMA, THE THINGS I COULD NEVER TELL STEVEN, JESUS WANTS ME FOR A SUNBEAM (Belvoir season). Training: National Institute of Dramatic Art: Production.

BELLA WELLSTEAD
ASSISTANT STAGE MANAGER

As production assistant: Ensemble Theatre: THE HEARTBREAK CHOIR, MCGUFFIN PARK, COLDER THAN HERE, THE QUEEN'S NANNY, UNCLE VANYA, MASTER CLASS, MR BAILEY'S MINDER. As set and costume design: Flight Path Theatre: THE ESCAPE ROOM. New Ghosts Theatre Company: FRAME NARRATIVE. As assistant director: New Theatre: ATLANTIS.

RENATA BESLIK
COSTUME SUPERVISOR

Ensemble Theatre: UNCLE VANYA, MASTER CLASS, ULSTER AMERICAN, SWITZERLAND, ALONE IT STANDS, THE GREAT DIVIDE, THE MEMORY OF WATER, SUMMER OF HAROLD, MR BAILEY'S MINDER, BENEFACTORS, RHINESTONE REX AND MISS MONICA, THE CARETAKER, PHOTOGRAPH 51, THE ONE, OUTDATED, CRUNCH TIME, BABY DOLL, FOLK, LUNA GALE, and many more. Bell Shakespeare: HENRY V, THE WINTER'S TALE, MACBETH. Belvoir St Theatre: FANGIRLS. New Theatricals: DARKNESS. National Institute of Dramatic Art: THE GOVERNMENT INSPECTOR, STAY HAPPY KEEP SMILING, THE TEMPEST, WOYCECK, A LIE OF THE MIND, PORT, THE THREESOME. Pinchgut Opera: JULIUS CAESAR, RINALDO, MÉDÉE, ORONTEA, PLATÉE and many more. Sydney Festival: BETTY BLOKKBUSTER RE-IMAGINED. Australian Chamber Orchestra: THE NUTCRACKER.

SUPPORT US

Every dollar counts. Ensemble relies on self-earned income to deliver all the programs that we do – commissioning new work, education outreach, producing world premieres, so please think about your capacity to make a gift to Ensemble. You can donate online at ensemble.com.au/support-us or contact Stephen Attfield, Philanthropy & Partnerships Manager, on **stephena@ensemble.com.au** or via **02 8918 3400.**

LIFE PATRONS

Those who have made significant contributions to Ensemble:
The Balnaves Foundation
Clitheroe Foundation
Jinnie & Ross Gavin
Ingrid Kaiser
Graham McConnochie
Neilson Foundation
Jenny Reynolds & Guy Reynolds AO
George & Diana Shirling
Southern Steel Group Pty Ltd

PLATINUM $20,000+

The Balnaves Foundation
Graham Bradley AM & Charlene Bradley
Clitheroe Foundation
Ingrid Kaiser
Graham McConnochie
Neilson Foundation
Alicia Powell
Jenny Reynolds & Guy Reynolds AO
Southern Steel Group Pty Ltd
Giving Support Foundation
Christine Thomson

GOLD $10,000+

Diane Balnaves
Darin Cooper Foundation
Jinnie & Ross Gavin
Steve & Julie Murphy
John & Diana Smythe Foundation
Jane Tham & Philip Maxwell

SILVER $5,000+

Debby Cramer & Bill Caukill
Peter Eichhorn & Anne Willems
Ellimo 2 Family Trust
APS Foundation - Brent & Vicki Emmett Giving Fund
Friends of Tracey Trinder
Garry, Debbie & Val
Alan Gunn & Kerri Fogg
Matilda Hartwell
Emma Hodgman & John Coorey

Anne Elizabeth King
Merryn & Rod Pearse
Alan & Pauline Plumb
David Pumphrey OAM & Jill Pumphrey
Angus & Elspeth Richards
Lynn Trainor
The Wenkart Foundation
Annie & Graham Williams
Liz Woolfson
Anonymous x 3

BRONZE $1,000+

Heather & Peter Andrews
Fiona Hopkins & Paul Bedbrook
Ellen Borda
Anne Bruning
Axel & Alexandra Buchner
Wayne Cahill
Alison Carmine
Lynette Casey & Patrica Zancanaro
Anne Clark
Valerie Crawford
Sue Donnelly
Peter Lowry AM & Dr Carolyn Lowry OAM
Hon Ben Franklin MLC
Vivienne Golis
Tim & Jill Golledge
Diane Grady & Christopher Komor
Andrew & Wendy Hamlin
Richard Hansford
Yvonne Hazell OAM
The Hilmer Family Endowment
Carolyn Hum
Jacqueline Katz
John Lewis
Michael Markiewicz
Catriona Morgan-Hunn
Barbara Osborne
Georgie Parker
In Memory of John Power
Jim & Maggie Pritchitt
Megan & Tim Sjoquist
Holly Stein

Bob Taffel
Geoffrey Tebbutt
Judy Thomson
Wendy Trevor Jones
Gai & Tony Wales
Geoffrey & Helen Webber
Dr Eric Wegman
Julia Wokes
Gavin M. Wong
In memory of John & Vanda Wright
Anonymous x 2

COMMISSIONERS' CIRCLE

Supporting new Australian work
Diane Balnaves
Graham Bradley AM & Charlene Bradley
Paul Clitheroe AM & Vicki Clitheroe
Jennifer Darin & Dennis Cooper
Ingrid Kaiser
Steve & Julie Murphy
Alicia Powell
Jenny Reynolds & Guy Reynolds AO
George & Diana Shirling
Jane Tham & Philip Maxwell
Christine Thomson

LEAVE A LEGACY

We would like to thank the following Estates for their generous donations
Estate of Freddie Bluhm
Estate of Jayati Dutta
Estate of Helen Gordon
Estate of Leo Mamontoff
Estates of Zika & Dimitry Nesteroff
Estate of Margaret Stenhouse

ENCORE CIRCLE

Thank you to the following people for bequests in their wills:
Liz Barton
Mark Midwinter
Joe Sbarro
Junia Vaz de Melo
Anonymous x 7

Supporters are recognized for 12 months from the date of donation. Current at 12 December 2024.

OUR PARTNERS

Thank you to our partners for playing a vital role in our success.

MAJOR PARTNER

ASSOCIATE PARTNER

NEILSON
FOUNDATION

STRATEGIC PARTNER

SOUTHERN
First for Steel

SUPPORTING PARTNERS

AKCS
www.akcs.com.au

AUDIO VISUAL EVENTS

BLOOMINGALES
LIFESTYLE STORE

Hungerford Hill

KH KAY & HUGHES

KENNARDS
HIRE

SPS. Sydney
Physio
Solutions

ENSEMBLE ED PARTNERS

Clitheroe
Foundation

S.B.W
foundation

The Smith
Family

everyone's family

ENSEMBLE AMBASSADORS

Thanks to our Ambassadors for their continued support.

TODD MCKENNEY   BRIAN MEEGAN   GEORGIE PARKER   KATE RAISON

ENSEMBLE THEATRE TEAM